Natural

Natural

WHOLESOME RECIPES
FOR PURE NOURISHMENT

Bath • New York • Cologne • Melbourne • Delhi
Hong Kong • Shenzhen • Singapore • Amsterdam

This edition published by Parragon Books Ltd in 2016 and distributed by

Parragon Inc.
440 Park Avenue South, 13th Floor
New York, NY 10016
www.parragon.com

ISBN 978-1-4723-9244-2
Printed in China

New recipes: Georgina Fuggle
Introduction text: Anne Sheasby
New recipe photography: Mike Cooper
Home economy: Lincoln Jefferson
Cover photography: Haarala Hamilton
Designer: Karli Skelton
Senior Editor: Cheryl Warner
Illustrations: Sarah Dennis, courtesy of New Division agency

NOTES FOR THE READER

This book uses standard kitchen measuring spoons and cups. All spoon and cup measurements are level unless otherwise indicated. Unless otherwise stated, milk is assumed to be whole, eggs are large, individual vegetables are medium, and pepper is freshly ground black pepper. Unless otherwise stated, all root vegetables should be peeled prior to using.

The times given are only an approximate guide. Preparation times differ according to the techniques used by different people and the cooking times may also vary from those given.

Garnishes, decorations, and serving suggestions are all optional and not necessarily included in the recipe ingredients or method. Any optional ingredients and seasoning to taste are not included in the nutritional analysis. The nutritional values given are approximate and provided as only a guideline; they do not account for an individual cook's abilities, imprecise measurements, and portion sizes.

Contents

INTRODUCTION 6

12

WAKE UP!

50

ENERGY-FUELING
LUNCHES

94

SUPERCHARGED
SNACKS & SIDES

126

DRESSINGS,
SAUCES & DIPS

152

A FEAST OF
VEGETABLES

196

POWER-PACKED
PROTEIN

240

THE SWEET STUFF

284

HEALTHY NECTARS

INDEX 316

The Natural Way

Fresh, natural, and simple ingredients play an important role in eating well and encourage a clean and health-giving approach to everyday eating. Incorporating more nutrient-dense foods and fewer processed ones into your everyday diet will also help to boost, balance, and benefit your overall health and happiness.

Forget fad diets and quick-fix weight-loss plans, because we have the perfect guide to healthy home cooking, the natural way. This inspiring and creative cookbook includes an amazing array of delicious, nutrient-rich recipes to help you feel more energized and revitalized, plus some hints and tips and savvy solutions for good, simple, natural eating. These recipes include plenty of fresh and natural ingredients, as well as a range of superfoods, making them perfect for the healthy home cook who wants to create tasty, nourishing, nutritionally balanced dishes that are ideal for everyday eating. We cater for all tastes and preferences, plus we feature some scrumptious sugar-free, gluten-free, and dairy-free options for those who need to avoid certain foods.

A healthy breakfast is important to get you off to a good start, because it boosts your energy levels in the morning and improves your ability to concentrate and perform. Therefore, to stimulate your senses first thing, we begin with a great choice of sustaining breakfast recipes, including the always popular pancakes, plus delicious blinis, baked eggs, oatmeal, muffins, and waffles.

Next, we focus on a tempting assortment of energy-packed lunches that are sure to hit the spot just when your stomach begins to rumble. Appetizing soups, superfood salads, flatbreads, frittatas, wraps, tarts, and quiches are all given the spotlight in this chapter.

When energy levels begin to flag during the day, why not turn to our next chapter to discover a savvy selection of supercharged snacks and sides? These are guaranteed to recharge and sustain you until your next meal. Top picks include popcorn, power balls, snacking nuts, roasted fries and wedges, not forgetting wonderful falafels and mashed carrots.

Delicious dressings and sauces follow next, and these are perfect for adding a beneficial health boost to vibrant salads and wholesome pasta dishes, plus we include some standout dips to enjoy, too.

A fabulous feast of versatile vegetable-loaded dishes includes choice cold and hot creations, featuring a range of vegetables, beans, rice, and pasta, as well as wholesome grains and seeds, such as farro and quinoa.

Power-packed protein dishes include a mouth-watering collection of healthy, balanced recipes from around the world, boasting nutrient-rich salads and stir-fries, hearty roasts and grills, plus some feel-good couscous creations.

A scrumptious selection of healthy desserts and baked items promises plenty of appealing recipes to satisfy sweet cravings. Temptations range from family favorites, such as brownies and cupcakes, to chilled or frozen sensations, such as cheesecakes, mousses, and sundaes.

Finally, to finish things off on a healthy high note, we showcase some nourishing nectars that are ideal for refreshing and revitalizing. We include invigorating juices, tonics, coolers, whips, and milk shakes, as well as some restorative teas and infusions.

Nourish and Cleanse

Explore the diverse selection of simple, natural, healthy foods that are readily available, and aim to include a good variety of these foods in your everyday eating plan. Include lean meats, white fish, oily fish, a variety of beans and legumes, plenty of fruit and vegetables (at least five different portions every day), some whole dairy foods as well as soy or other dairy-free alternatives, whole grains, rice, pasta, eggs, nuts, and seeds. Herbs and spices add an arsenal of clean, natural flavors to many dishes, too.

Aim to eat an assortment of different fruits and vegetables in different colors, including a number of those high in antioxidants, such as beets, berries (for example, blackberries, blueberries, and raspberries), broccoli, cherries, kale, red grapes, red bell peppers, spinach, tomatoes, and so on.

Healthier choices of grains include fiber-rich brown rice, whole-wheat pasta, whole-grain flours, and whole-wheat bread. Occasionally, opt for something different, such as barley, buckwheat, quinoa, and farro, to add interest and variety to your meals.

Nuts are packed with protein, plus they provide a variety of valuable vitamins and minerals, and although nuts are typically high in fat, the fats tend to be the more healthy unsaturated types. Seeds, such as pumpkin, sunflower, sesame, chia, and flaxseed, add a nourishing nutrient boost to dishes, too. For the sweet stuff, choose unbleached sugars instead of refined ones, if you can.

If you are a meat or fish eater, then choose leaner cuts of meat and poultry and include both white fish and oily fish in your diet (oily fish are an excellent source of omega-3 fatty acids).

For vegetarians, beans and legumes provide an important source of protein, as well as fiber and vital vitamins and minerals, and a good range of dried, canned, fresh, and frozen ones are readily available. Or, if you want to eat less meat and prefer meat-light or meat-free days, then beans and legumes are great for bulking out dishes, such as casseroles, soups, and salads.

For health-conscious eaters, cooking from scratch really lends itself to natural home cooking, because it enables you to select the ingredients you want to use. Be label-aware, however, and become a savvy shopper, because even with homemade food, some ingredients may be processed. Certain processed foods can be eaten as part of a healthy, natural diet (for example, canned vegetables and beans without added sugar and sodium), but many processed foods contain added sugar, sodium, and fat (especially saturated fat) in varying amounts. So before you go shopping and make your choices, check out the general guidelines readily available and get accustomed to checking the labels before you buy.

This appealing collection of flavorful, wholesome recipes will inspire and spur you on to embrace a healthy, natural, and balanced approach to eating for improved overall vitality and well-being. We include plenty of delicious and satisfying recipes for all tastes that will effortlessly slip into a nourishing everyday diet, so you can easily enjoy cooking and eating delicious, feel-good food packed full of fresh flavor and appeal.

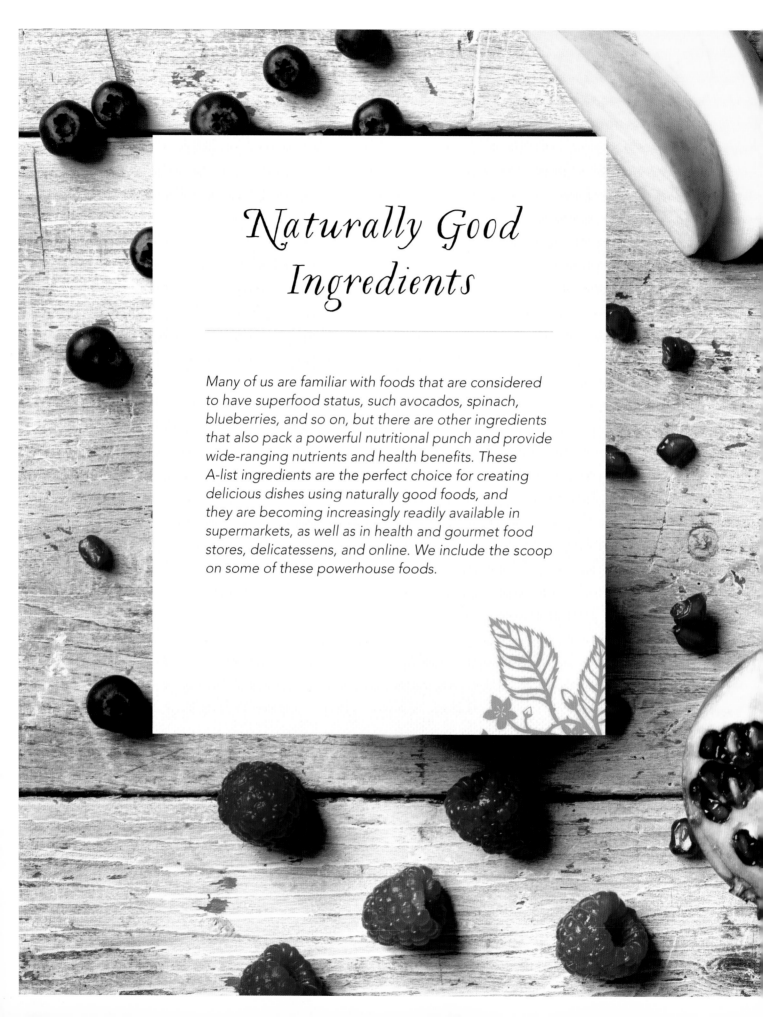

Naturally Good Ingredients

Many of us are familiar with foods that are considered to have superfood status, such avocados, spinach, blueberries, and so on, but there are other ingredients that also pack a powerful nutritional punch and provide wide-ranging nutrients and health benefits. These A-list ingredients are the perfect choice for creating delicious dishes using naturally good foods, and they are becoming increasingly readily available in supermarkets, as well as in health and gourmet food stores, delicatessens, and online. We include the scoop on some of these powerhouse foods.

Almond milk Made by toasting or roasting whole almonds, then grinding them and blending with water. A dairy-free alternative to traditional dairy milk; naturally low in fat, lactose-free, gluten-free, and cholesterol-free.

Beets Deep, red beets are the most common type, but pink, golden, and striped beets are also available. Low in fat and packed full of vitamins, minerals, and antioxidants; good source of fiber.

Buckwheat Comprising grain-like triangular seeds (that are no relation to cereal wheat) with a nutty flavor; can be used toasted or plain, as whole seeds, or ground into flour. Good source of protein and fiber; naturally gluten-free and wheat-free.

Chia seeds Tiny, oval, mottled brown/gray seeds. Natural, rich, gluten-free source of omega-3 fatty acids; good source of vitamins, minerals, protein, and fiber.

Coconut oil Very high in saturated fats, but the type of saturated fatty acids it contains (which differ from those typically found in animal products) are considered to be "good" saturated fats. However, use in moderation.

Coconut water Clear liquid extracted from the inside of young green coconuts. A good source of important vitamins and minerals, including potassium; low in calories and fat (and cholesterol-free).

Flaxseed Small, pale brown or golden seeds; also known as linseeds. Naturally gluten-free; rich source of omega-3 essential fatty acids and good source of fiber.

Goji berries Small, dried, vibrant red berries; contain a variety of valuable vitamins and minerals, including antioxidants.

Kale Member of cabbage family. Hardy, deep green, leafy winter vegetable with strong flavor; available as smooth-leaved kale or crinkly-leaved curly kale. Excellent source of various vitamins and minerals, including vitamin C.

Medjool dates Large, fleshy dates imported from the Middle East and North Africa; available all year round. Low in fat and sodium; good source of fiber. High natural sugar content.

Pomegranate Inside the hard, red-blushed skin are numerous edible seeds, each one surrounded by a sac of sweet, juicy, vibrant pink flesh (packed in bitter white pith). Low in fat; good source of fiber, antioxidant vitamins, and minerals.

Quinoa Ancient grain-like seed from South America. Tiny, round, bead-shape seeds, available in three main types (red, creamy white/pale golden, and black); swell as they cook and have a mild, nutty taste. Complete protein food (contains all essential amino acids). Good gluten-free source of protein, fiber, and minerals.

Spirulina Blue-green natural freshwater algae, rich in protein (complete protein food—contains all essential amino acids) and other nutrients, including various vitamins and minerals. Available as a nutrient-dense powder (or pills).

Wheatgrass Available fresh or as a juice or powder. Fresh wheatgrass is grown from sprouted wheatgrass seeds or wheat berries; vibrant green with a strong, sweet, grass-like flavor. Natural, rich source of vitamins and minerals, including antioxidants.

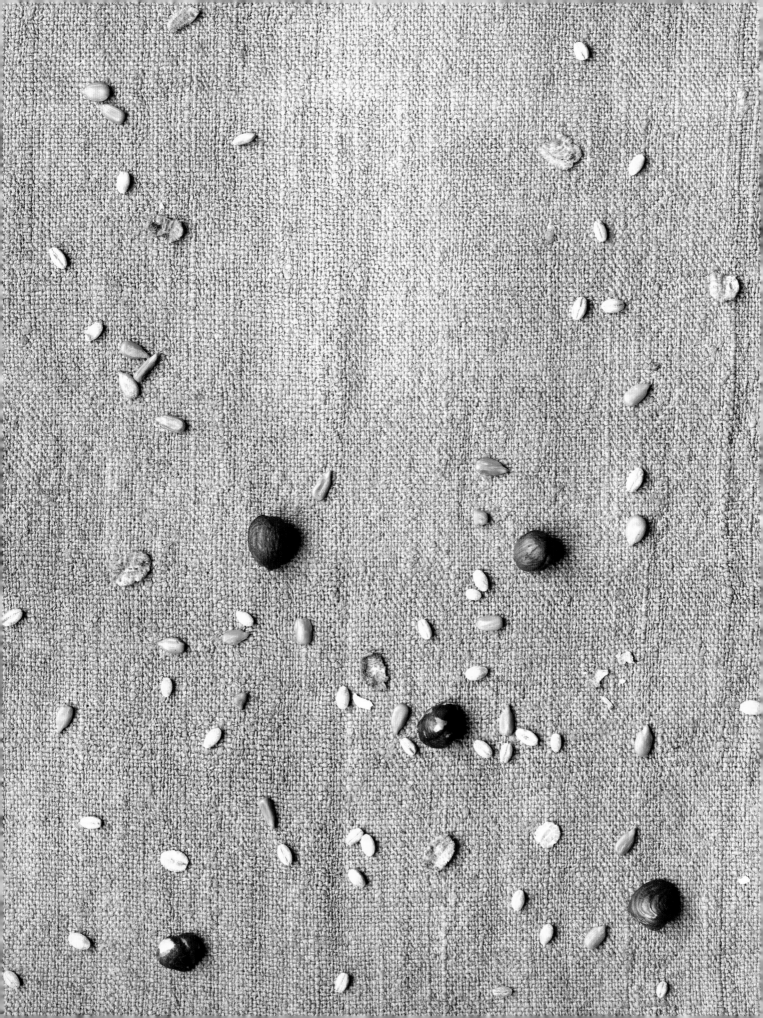

Wake Up!

Barley Porridge with Carmelized Fruits

This maca-enriched creamy barley porridge is made with almond milk and topped with cinnamon-caramelized fresh peaches and papaya. It is then drizzled with honey to create this tasty, dairy-free breakfast.

Serves 4

Prep: 15 minutes
Cook: 10–15 minutes

2 cups barley flakes
1 cup rolled oats
1½ cups cold water
3 cups unsweetened almond milk
4 teaspoons maca powder
2 peaches, halved, pitted, and sliced
1 papaya, halved, seeded, peeled, and sliced
4 teaspoons honey
½ teaspoon ground cinnamon
2 teaspoons honey, to serve

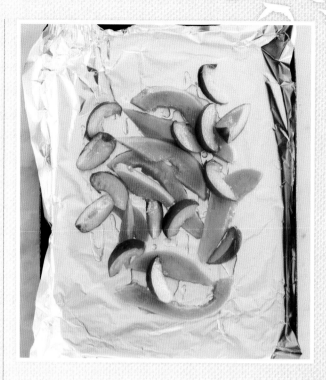

1. Put the barley flakes, rolled oats, water, and almond milk into a saucepan. Bring to a boil over medium–high heat, then reduce the heat to medium and simmer for 5–10 minutes, stirring often, until soft and thickened. Stir in the maca powder.

2. Meanwhile, preheat the broiler to medium–high. Line the broiler rack with aluminum foil, then lay the peaches and papaya on top, drizzle with the honey, and sprinkle with the cinnamon. Broil for 3–4 minutes, or until hot and just beginning to caramelize.

3. Spoon the porridge into bowls, top with the hot peaches and papaya, and drizzle with the honey.

Greek-Style Yogurt with Orange Zest & Toasted Seeds

Serves 2

Prep: 10 minutes, plus cooling
Cook: 2–3 minutes

2 teaspoons flaxseed

2 teaspoons pumpkin seeds

2 teaspoons chia seeds

1 cup Greek-style plain yogurt

grated zest of 1 small orange,
  plus 1 teaspoon juice

A nutritious assortment of seeds add extra crunch, flavor, and color to these quick-and-easy, low-sugar yogurt treats.

1. Put a small skillet over medium heat. When it is hot, add the seeds. Toast, stirring constantly with a wooden spoon, until they start to turn brown and release a nutty aroma. Transfer to a plate and let cool.

2. Spoon the yogurt into two small serving dishes or even jars, then sprinkle the seeds on top, followed by the orange zest. Sprinkle with the orange juice and serve immediately.

PER SERVING: *152 cal / 8.9g fat / 4g sat fat / 7.7g carbs / 4.1g sugar / 2.7g fiber / 11.1g protein / 40mg sodium*

Healthy French Toast with Bananas & Toasted Pecans

Serves 4
Prep: 20 minutes
Cook: 12–17 minutes

½ cup coarsely chopped pecans
2 eggs
4 ripe bananas, chopped
½ teaspoon vanilla extract
½ teaspoon ground cinnamon
4 thick slices whole-wheat bread
1 tablespoon olive oil
½ teaspoon ground cinnamon, to sprinkle

There's no better way to start the day than with this tempting, sustaining banana-and-nut-topped French toast.

1. Put the pecans into a small, dry skillet and toast over medium heat for 3–4 minutes, tossing regularly until just toasted. Set aside.

2. Put the eggs, two of the bananas, the vanilla extract, and cinnamon into a blender and process for 1–2 minutes, or until the consistency is smooth and thick.

3. Pour the mixture into a medium, shallow dish. Place two slices of bread into the mixture and, working quickly, gently press the bread into the liquid, letting it soak up the mixture. Turn the slices over and repeat.

4. Meanwhile, heat half of the olive oil in a large, nonstick skillet over medium–high heat. Using a spatula, remove the soaked bread from the banana mixture and place in the skillet. Cook for 2–3 minutes on each side before removing from the pan. Repeat the process with the remaining slices, adding the remaining olive oil, if needed.

5. Serve the banana bread immediately, with a sprinkling of cinnamon and topped with the toasted pecans and remaining two chopped bananas.

PER SERVING: *405 cal / 19.4g fat / 2.7g sat fat / 53.4g carbs / 17g sugar / 7.6g fiber / 9.7g protein / 200mg sodium*

Seed-Packed Granola

For a satisfying start to the day, try this great-tasting granola, piled with healthy cinnamon-toasted, whole-grain oats and seeds and combined with fiber-rich dried fruits. Make ahead, because it keeps for a few days, too.

Serves 6
Prep: 20 minutes, plus cooling and storing
Cook: 30–35 minutes

1¾ cups rolled oats

¼ cup pumpkin seeds

¼ cup sunflower seeds

¼ cup sesame seeds

1 teaspoon ground cinnamon

2 tablespoons packed light brown sugar

2 tablespoons olive oil

2 tablespoons honey

juice of 1 small orange

½ cup diced dried apple slices

⅓ cup dried blueberries

⅓ cup dried cranberries

1. Preheat the oven to 325°F. Add the rolled oats, pumpkin seeds, sunflower seeds, and sesame seeds to a 7 x 11-inch roasting pan. Sprinkle with the cinnamon and sugar, then stir together.

2. Drizzle the oil, honey, and orange juice over the top and mix together. Bake in the preheated oven for 30–35 minutes, stirring after 15 minutes and moving the mixture in the corners to the center, because the edges brown more quickly. Try to keep the granola in clumps. Return to the oven and stir every 5–10 minutes, until the granola is an even, golden brown.

3. Sprinkle the dried apple, blueberries, and cranberries over the top and let the granola cool and harden. Serve or spoon into a plastic container or canning jar and store in the refrigerator for up to four days.

PER SERVING: *357 cal / 16.3g fat / 2.3g sat fat / 48.4g carbs / 23.3g sugar / 6.2g fiber / 8.2g protein / trace sodium*

Spinach & Nutmeg Baked Eggs

Serves 4

Prep: 20 minutes, plus cooling
Cook: 20–30 minutes

1 tablespoon olive oil, for brushing
1 tablespoon olive oil, for frying
4 shallots, finely chopped
3 garlic cloves, sliced
3½ cups baby spinach
8 eggs
½ teaspoon ground nutmeg
salt and pepper, optional

Nutrient-rich fresh spinach adds delicious flavor and color to this popular egg dish, lightly seasoned with ground nutmeg. Serve with standard or gluten-free bread for a wholesome breakfast or brunch.

1. Preheat the oven to 350°F. Lightly brush the insides of four 1-cup ramekins (individual ceramic dishes) with olive oil.

2. Heat the olive oil in a skillet. Once hot, add the shallots and garlic and sauté over medium heat for 3–4 minutes, or until soft. Add the baby spinach and stir for 2–3 minutes, or until just wilted. Season with salt and pepper, if using.

3. Spoon the spinach mixture into the bottom of the prepared ramekins and crack two eggs into each. Sprinkle with the nutmeg and place the ramekins in a roasting pan. Fill the roasting pan with boiling water until the water reaches halfway up the ramekins; this creates a steamy environment for the eggs so there will be no chance for them to dry out.

4. Carefully transfer the roasting pan to the preheated oven for 15–20 minutes. Let the ramekins cool slightly, then serve immediately.

PER SERVING: *235 cal / 16.5g fat / 4.2g sat fat / 7.5g carbs / 1.6g sugar / 1.1g fiber / 14.2g protein / 160mg sodium*

Cinnamon Crepes with Tropical Fruit Salad

Using soy milk for these tasty whole-wheat crepes, and serving them with soy yogurt, makes them both delicious and dairy-free. Naturally sweet ripe pineapple and mango mean no sugar is necessary for the fruit salad.

Serves 4
Prep: 30 minutes
Cook: 30 minutes

¾ cup whole-wheat flour
½ teaspoon ground cinnamon
2 eggs, beaten
1 cup unsweetened soy milk
3 tablespoons water
3 tablespoons sunflower oil

Fruit salad
1 ruby grapefruit
1½ cups pineapple chunks
1 cup mango chunks
finely grated zest of ½ lime

To serve
1⅓ cups plain soy yogurt
2 tablespoons date syrup
12 Brazil nuts, coarsely chopped, optional

1. For the fruit salad, cut the peel and pith away from the grapefruit with a small serrated knife. Hold it above a bowl and cut between the membranes to release the sections into the bowl. Squeeze the juice from the membranes into the bowl. Add the pineapple, mango, and lime zest and mix well.

2. For the pancakes, put the flour and cinnamon into another bowl. Add the eggs, then gradually whisk in the soy milk until smooth. Whisk in the water and 1 tablespoon of oil.

PER SERVING: *369 cal / 16.2g fat / 2.4g sat fat / 45.9g carbs / 22.3g sugar / 6.4g fiber / 12.5g protein / 120mg sodium*

3. Heat a little oil in a 7-inch skillet over medium heat, then pour out the excess oil. Pour in one-eighth of the batter, tilting the pan to swirl the batter into an even layer. Cook for 2 minutes, or until the underside is golden.

4. Loosen the thin pancake, then flip it over with a spatula and cook the second side for 1 minute, or until golden. Slide the thin pancake out of the pan and keep hot on a plate while you make another seven thin pancakes in the same way.

5. Arrange two folded pancakes on each of four plates and top with the fruit salad. Serve with the soy yogurt and drizzle with the date syrup. Top with the Brazil nuts, if using.

Breakfast Carrot Cake Cookies

Makes 12

Prep: 25–30 minutes
Cook: 16–19 minutes

½ cup plus 1 tablespoon flaxseed
¾ cup whole-wheat flour
¾ cup rolled oats
1 teaspoon baking powder
1 teaspoon ground ginger
2 teaspoons ground cinnamon
½ cup finely chopped dried apricots
1 sweet, crisp apple, such as
 Golden Delicious or Pink Lady,
 cored and coarsely grated
1 carrot, finely grated
⅓ cup coarsely chopped pecans
3 tablespoons coconut oil
½ cup maple syrup
grated zest of ½ orange,
 plus 3 tablespoons juice
¼ cup dried coconut shavings

Full of nutrient-loaded seeds, oats, nuts, carrots, and fruit, these lightly spiced, zesty cookies pack a fantastic flavor punch, as well as being great for energy. They are perfect for breakfast on the run, because they can be made ahead, too.

1. Preheat the oven to 350°F and line two baking sheets with parchment paper.

2. Put the flaxseed into a blender and process to a fine powder, then transfer to a mixing bowl. Add the flour, oats, and baking powder, then the ginger and cinnamon, and stir well. Add the dried apricots, apple, carrot, and pecans and stir again.

3. Warm the coconut oil in a small saucepan (or in the microwave for 30 seconds) until just liquid. Remove from the heat, then stir in the maple syrup and orange zest and juice. Pour this into the carrot mixture and stir until you have a soft dough.

4. Spoon 12 mounds of the dough onto the prepared baking sheets, then flatten them into thick 3-inch diameter circles. Sprinkle with the coconut shavings, then bake in the preheated oven for 15–18 minutes, or until browned.

5. Serve warm or let cool, then pack into a plastic container and store in the refrigerator for up to three days.

PER COOKIE: *212 cal / 11.2g fat / 4.7g sat fat / 27g carbs / 12.4g sugar / 5.5g fiber / 4.1g protein / 40mg sodium*

Three Herb & Ricotta Omelet

Vibrant green, mixed fresh herbs add plenty of wonderful natural flavor and color to this appetizing omelet. Served with fresh bread to accompany, it's just the ticket for a satisfying breakfast for two.

Serves 2
Prep: 15 minutes
Cook: 8 minutes

4 extra-large eggs
2 tablespoons finely snipped fresh chives
2 tablespoons finely chopped fresh basil
2 tablespoons finely chopped fresh parsley
⅓ cup plus 1 tablespoon ricotta cheese
2 tablespoons olive oil
salt and pepper, optional

1. Crack the eggs into a small mixing bowl and lightly beat with a fork. Stir the herbs and ricotta into the bowl and season with salt and pepper, if using.

2. Heat the olive oil in a nonstick skillet over high heat until hot. Pour in the egg mixture and, using a spatula, draw the outside edges (which will cook more quickly) toward the gooey center. Let any liquid mixture move into the gaps. Continue with this action for 4–5 minutes. The omelet will continue to cook once the pan is removed from the heat.

3. Cut the omelet in half and divide between two plates. Serve immediately.

PER SERVING: *390 cal / 32g fat / 10g sat fat / 2.8g carbs / 0.7g sugar / 0.2g fiber / 21.7g protein / 240mg sodium*

Homemade Cacao & Hazelnut Butter

Makes 1¼ cups
Prep: 15 minutes, plus standing
Cook: 3–4 minutes

¾ cup plus 2 tablespoons
    unblanched hazelnuts
⅓ cup raw cacao powder
⅓ cup firmly packed light brown sugar
½ cup light olive oil
½ teaspoon vanilla extract
pinch of sea salt
whole-grain toast or pancakes,
    to serve, optional

Spread on hot whole-grain toast, this healthy hazelnut butter is delicious for breakfast, plus it keeps well for several days.

1. Add the hazelnuts to a dry skillet and cook over medium heat for 3–4 minutes, constantly shaking the pan, until the nuts are an even golden brown.

2. Wrap the nuts in a clean dish towel and rub to remove the skins.

3. Put the nuts into a blender and blend until finely ground. Add the cacao powder, sugar, oil, vanilla extract, and salt, and blend again to make a smooth paste.

4. Spoon into a small airtight jar and seal. Let stand at room temperature for 4 hours, until the sugar has dissolved completely. Stir again, then store in the refrigerator for up to five days. Serve on whole-grain toast or hot pancakes, if desired.

PER 1¼ CUPS: *2206 cal / 197.7g fat / 24.2g sat fat / 104.3g carbs / 73.2g sugar / 18.3g fiber / 22.7g protein / 600mg sodium*

Cardamom Waffles with Blackberries & Figs

Aromatic cardamom adds a wonderful depth of flavor to these fabulous fruit-topped waffles, so dig out your waffle maker and cook up this satisfying weekend family breakfast when late-summer blackberries are at their best.

Serves 6

Prep: 25 minutes, plus resting
Cook: 10–17 minutes

5 extra-large eggs, separated
pinch of salt
1 teaspoon ground cardamom
3½ tablespoons unsalted butter, melted and cooled
1 cup low-fat milk
1¾ cups plus 2 tablespoons whole-wheat flour
1 tablespoon olive oil, for brushing
⅔ cup Greek-style plain yogurt
6 ripe figs, quartered
1⅓ cups blackberries
⅓ cup agave syrup, to serve

1. Put the egg yolks, salt, and cardamom into a bowl and beat well with a wooden spoon. Stir in the melted butter. Slowly beat in the milk until completely incorporated. Gradually add the flour until you have a thick batter.

2. In a separate bowl, whisk the egg whites until they form stiff peaks and gently fold them into the batter. Let the batter rest for at least an hour, but preferably overnight.

3. Heat the waffle maker according to the manufacturer's directions. Brush with a little oil and spoon the batter onto the waffle iron. Cook for 4–5 minutes, or until golden. Keep each waffle warm, under aluminum foil and in a low oven, until you are ready to serve.

4. Serve each waffle immediately, topped with yogurt, fig quarters, blackberries, and agave syrup.

PER SERVING: *422 cal / 17.3g fat / 7.8g sat fat / 53.9g carbs / 23.7g sugar / 7.3g fiber / 16.1g protein / 200mg sodium*

Pumpkin & Pepita Muffins

Makes 12

Prep: 25–30 minutes, plus cooling
Cook: 30 minutes

1 tablespoon light olive oil, for greasing
2 cups finely diced, peeled, and seeded
   pumpkin or butternut squash
1½-inch piece fresh ginger,
   coarsely grated
3 eggs
¼ cup maple syrup
1 cup low-fat plain yogurt
1¼ cups whole-wheat flour
¾ cup fine cornmeal
1 tablespoon baking powder
1 teaspoon ground allspice
3 tablespoons pepita (pumpkin) seeds

Dark, olive green pepita seeds from pumpkins add crunch and a mild nutty flavor to these delicious muffins. They are ideal for an energy-boosting breakfast or brunch and are great as a midmorning snack.

1. Preheat the oven to 375°F. Grease a 12-cup muffin pan with the oil.

2. Put the pumpkin into the top of a steamer set over a saucepan of gently simmering water. Cover and cook for 15 minutes, or until just soft. Mash the pumpkin and mix with the grated ginger.

3. Put the eggs, maple syrup, and yogurt into a medium bowl and whisk together.

4. Put the flour, cornmeal, baking powder, and allspice into a large bowl and stir together. Add the mashed pumpkin and the egg mixture and briefly beat together until just combined.

5. Spoon the batter evenly into the cups of the prepared pan. Sprinkle the tops of the muffins with the seeds, then bake in the preheated oven for 15 minutes, or until well risen and golden brown. Let cool in the pan for 5 minutes, then loosen the edges with a knife. Turn out onto a wire rack and let cool completely.

PER MUFFIN: *150 cal / 4.2g fat / 1g sat fat / 23.7g carbs / 5.9g sugar / 1.9g fiber / 5.7g protein / 160mg sodium*

Red Beet Hash

Serves 4
Prep: 25–30 minutes
Cook: 45 minutes

12 ounces Jerusalem artichokes,
    unpeeled and scrubbed

5–6 raw beets (1 pound), cut into cubes

5 sweet potatoes (1 pound 10 ounces),
    cut into cubes

2 tablespoons olive oil

1 red onion, coarsely chopped

2 teaspoons mild paprika

½ teaspoon dry mustard

1 tablespoon fresh thyme leaves

4 eggs

salt and pepper, optional

1 teaspoon fresh thyme
    leaves, to garnish

Piled with health-giving nutrients, fresh beets add wonderful color and flavor to this wholesome root vegetable hash, topped with protein-rich eggs. An ideal meat-free weekend breakfast or brunch for the whole family.

1. Halve any of the larger artichokes. Fill the bottom of a steamer halfway with water, bring to a boil, then add the artichokes to the water. Put the beets into one half of the steamer top, cover with a lid, and steam for 10 minutes.

2. Put the sweet potatoes into the other half of the top, so the color of the beets doesn't bleed into the sweet potatoes. Cover with a lid again and steam for an additional 10 minutes, or until all the vegetables are just tender. Drain the artichokes, peel them, and cut them into cubes.

3. Heat 1 tablespoon of oil in a large skillet over medium heat. Add the red onion and sauté for 3–4 minutes, or until beginning to soften. Add the artichokes, beets, and sweet potatoes and sauté for 10 minutes, or until browned.

4. Stir in the paprika, dry mustard, and thyme and season with salt and pepper, if using. Make four spaces in the skillet, drizzle in the remaining oil, then crack an egg into each hole. Sprinkle the eggs with salt and pepper, if using, then cover and cook for 4–5 minutes, or until the eggs are cooked to your preference. Spoon onto plates and serve immediately, garnished with the thyme.

PER SERVING: *426 cal / 12.1g fat / 2.6g sat fat / 68.5g carbs / 25.7g sugar / 11.3g fiber / 13.4g protein / 240mg sodium*

Mushrooms on Rye Toast

Simple to make, yet tasty, these mixed fresh mushrooms are pan-fried with garlic, then served on top of toasted rye bread, creating a quick-and-easy breakfast that will get you off to a good start in the morning.

Serves 4

Prep: 15 minutes
Cook: 10 minutes

3 tablespoons olive oil
2 large garlic cloves, crushed
8 ounces cremini mushrooms, sliced
8 ounces wild mushrooms, sliced
2 teaspoons lemon juice
2 tablespoons finely chopped fresh flat-leaf parsley
4 slices of rye bread
sea salt and pepper, optional

1. Heat the oil in a large skillet over medium–low heat. Add the garlic and cook for a few seconds.

2. Increase the heat to high. Add the cremini mushrooms to the pan and sauté, stirring continuously, for 3 minutes. Add the wild mushrooms and sauté for an additional 2 minutes.

3. Stir in the lemon juice and parsley, and season with salt and pepper, if using.

4. Lightly toast the rye bread, then transfer to a serving plate. Spoon the mushroom mixture over the toast and serve immediately.

PER SERVING: *206 cal / 11.6g fat / 1.6g sat fat / 21.8g carbs / 2.6g sugar / 3.9g fiber / 6.1g protein / 360mg sodium*

Buckwheat Blinis with Pears & Blueberries

Serves 4

Prep: 30 minutes, plus rising
Cook: 20–27 minutes

1½ cups buckwheat flour

½ teaspoon sea salt

2 teaspoons packed dark brown sugar

1 teaspoon active dry yeast

½ cup milk

½ cup water

1 tablespoon virgin olive oil

Topping

2 tablespoons unsalted butter

2 pears, cored and thickly sliced

1 cup blueberries

2 tablespoons honey

juice of ½ lemon

1 cup Greek-style plain yogurt

pinch of ground cinnamon

3 tablespoons toasted unblanched
   hazelnuts, coarsely chopped

Superfood blueberries are a rich source of antioxidants and, when cooked lightly with pears, they provide a tasty topping for these naturally gluten-free buckwheat blinis. Greek-style yogurt and toasted hazelnuts complete this healthy breakfast perfectly.

1. To make the blinis, put the flour, salt, sugar, and yeast into a large bowl and mix together well. Put the milk and water into a small saucepan and gently heat until just warm. Gradually whisk the milk mixture into the flour until you have a smooth, thick batter.

2. Cover the bowl with a large plate and let rise in a warm place for 40–60 minutes, or until bubbles appear on the surface and the batter is almost doubled in size.

3. Heat half of the oil in a large flat griddle pan or skillet over medium heat. Remove the pan from the heat briefly and wipe away excess oil using paper towels. Return the pan to the heat and drop tablespoonfuls of the batter into it, leaving a little space between them. Cook for 2–3 minutes, or until the undersides are golden and the tops are beginning to bubble.

4. Turn the blinis over with a spatula and cook for another 1–2 minutes. Transfer to a baking sheet and keep warm in a low oven while you make the rest. Continue wiping the pan with oiled paper towels between cooking batches.

5. To make the topping, melt the butter in a skillet over medium heat. Add the fruit and cook for 2–3 minutes, or until hot. Drizzle with the honey and lemon juice and cook for 1 minute, or until the blueberry juices begin to run.

6. Arrange three blinis on each of four plates, top with spoonfuls of the yogurt, the hot fruit, a little ground cinnamon, and the hazelnuts. Serve immediately.

PER SERVING: 435 cal / 17g fat / 6.4g sat fat / 64.1g carbs / 27.1g sugar / 8.5g fiber / 13g protein / 320mg sodium

Poached Eggs & Kale with Whole-Wheat Sourdough

Serves 4
Prep: 20 minutes
Cook: 15–17 minutes

4 eggs
1½ cups chopped kale
4 large slices whole-wheat
　　sourdough bread
2 garlic cloves, chopped into halves
2 tablespoons olive oil
1 teaspoon crushed red pepper flakes
salt and pepper, optional

Kale adds valuable nutrients and vivid green color to these protein-packed poached eggs served on sensational sourdough toast.

1. Begin by poaching the eggs. Bring a shallow saucepan of water to a gentle simmer. Crack an egg into a small bowl, then slide the egg into the water, lowering the bowl as close to the water as possible. Using a large spoon, gently fold any stray strands of white around the yolk. Repeat with the other eggs.

2. Cook for 2–3 minutes, or until set to your preference, then remove with a slotted spoon. Place the eggs in a small bowl of warm water so they can sit until needed.

3. Bring a saucepan of water to a boil and add the kale. Simmer for 3–4 minutes, or until the kale is just cooked but still retains a little crunch. Drain, season with salt and pepper, if using, and set aside.

4. Meanwhile, toast the sourdough bread. Place the toast on four plates, then rub each slice with the raw garlic and drizzle with the olive oil. Top the toast with the blanched kale and a poached egg. Finally, sprinkle with crushed red pepper flakes. Serve immediately.

PER SERVING: *324 cal / 15.1g fat / 3g sat fat / 36.3g carbs / 2.6g sugar / 4.4g fiber / 12.6g protein / 400mg sodium*

Banana, Goji & Hazelnut Bread

Bananas are a storehouse of beneficial nutrients, so when you want to feel energized first thing, try this healthy, high-fiber breakfast loaf packed with bananas and dotted with nutritious goji berries and hazelnuts throughout.

Serves 10

Prep: 25 minutes, plus cooling
Cook: 50–60 minutes

½ tablespoon butter, for greasing
6 tablespoons butter, softened
½ cup firmly packed light brown sugar
2 eggs
4 bananas (about 1 pound), peeled and mashed
1 cup whole-wheat flour
1 cup white all-purpose flour
2 teaspoons baking powder
½ cup coarsely chopped unblanched hazelnuts
½ cup goji berries
⅔ cup dried banana chips

1. Preheat the oven to 350°F. Grease a 9 x 5 x 3-inch loaf pan and line the bottom and two long sides with a piece of parchment paper.

2. Cream the butter and sugar together in a large bowl. Beat in the eggs, one at a time, then the bananas.

3. Put the flours and baking powder into a bowl and mix well. Add to the banana mixture and beat until smooth. Add the hazelnuts and goji berries and stir well.

4. Spoon the batter into the prepared pan, smooth the top flat, then sprinkle with the banana chips. Bake for 50–60 minutes, or until the loaf is well risen, has cracked slightly, and a toothpick comes out cleanly when inserted into the center.

5. Let cool for 5 minutes, then loosen the edges with a blunt knife and turn out onto a wire rack. Let cool completely, then peel away the paper. Store in an airtight container for up to three days.

PER SERVING: *300 cal / 12.8g fat / 5.6g sat fat / 43.4g carbs / 19.3g sugar / 3.7g fiber / 5.9g protein / 160mg sodium*

Walnut & Seed Bread

Makes 2 large loaves

Prep: 30–35 minutes,
  plus rising and cooling
Cook: 25–30 minutes

4¼ cups whole-wheat flour

3⅔ cups white all-purpose flour

¾ cup plus 1 tablespoon
  white bread flour

½ cup plus 1 tablespoon malted
  wheat flakes

2½ tablespoons malt powder

2 tablespoons sesame seeds

2 tablespoons sunflower seeds

2 tablespoons poppy seeds

1 cup chopped walnuts

2 teaspoons salt

4½ teaspoons active dry yeast

2 tablespoons walnut oil

3 cups lukewarm water

2 tablespoons strong white flour,
  for dusting

1 tablespoon butter, melted, for greasing

Wholesome walnuts and scrumptious seeds add top flavor and crunch to this tempting whole-grain loaf. It's good served thickly sliced and spread with a little honey or soft cheese for a filling, healthy breakfast.

1. Put the flours, wheat flakes, malt powder, seeds, walnuts, salt, and yeast into a bowl and mix together. Make a well in the center, add the oil and water, and stir well to form a soft dough. Turn out the dough onto a lightly floured surface and knead well for 5–7 minutes, or until smooth and elastic.

2. Return the dough to the bowl, cover with a damp dish towel, and let rise in a warm place for 1–1½ hours, or until doubled in size. Turn out onto a lightly floured surface and knead again for 1 minute.

3. Brush two 9 x 5 x 3-inch loaf pans well with the melted butter. Divide the dough in two. Shape one piece about the same length of the pan and three times the width. Fold the dough in three lengthwise and place in one of the pans with the seam underneath. Repeat with the other piece of dough.

4. Cover and let rise again in a warm place for about 30 minutes, or until well risen above the tins. Meanwhile, preheat the oven to 450°F.

5. Bake the loaves in the center of the oven for 25–30 minutes. If the loaves are getting too brown, reduce the temperature to 425°F. Transfer to wire racks to cool.

PER LOAF: 3053 cal / 83.8g fat / 12.4g sat fat / 480g carbs / 12g sugar / 52g fiber / 114g protein / 2440mg sodium

Energy-Fueling Lunches

Mashed Avocado & Quinoa Wrap

Brimming with nourishing, natural goodness, fresh avocado and spinach combine with colorful, crunchy, raw red cabbage to create these really appealing quinoa-topped wraps. Great for sharing, because everyone can assemble their own.

Serves 4

Prep: 20 minutes, plus cooling
Cook: 15–18 minutes

1 cup quinoa
1¾ cups vegetable broth
1 large, ripe avocado, peeled and pitted
½ teaspoon smoked paprika
2 garlic cloves, crushed
grated zest and juice of 1 lemon
4 whole-wheat tortillas
1¾ cups baby spinach
1½ cups finely sliced red cabbage
salt and pepper, optional

1. Put the quinoa and vegetable broth into a small saucepan and simmer, covered, for 15–18 minutes, or until the broth has been completely absorbed. Set aside to cool.

2. Meanwhile, gently mash the avocado flesh with the smoked paprika, crushed garlic, lemon zest, and just enough lemon juice to make a thick consistency.

3. Spread the mashed avocado down the center of each wrap and then top with the warm quinoa, spinach, and red cabbage. Season with salt and pepper, if using. Tuck in the ends and tightly fold or roll into a wrap and serve immediately.

PER SERVING: *385 cal / 13.2g fat / 2.8g sat fat / 56.8g carbs / 3.6g sugar / 10.4g fiber / 11.8g protein / 560mg sodium*

Supergreen Salad

Prep: 20–25 minutes
Cook: 10–14 minutes

2 tablespoons pumpkin seeds
2 tablespoons sunflower seeds
2 tablespoons sesame seeds
4 teaspoons soy sauce
3½ cups broccoli florets
3 cups baby spinach
¾ cup thinly shredded kale
⅓ cup coarsely chopped fresh cilantro
2 avocados, sliced
juice of 2 limes

Dressing

3 tablespoons flaxseed oil
2 teaspoons honey
pepper, optional

This vibrant, green superfood salad is sure to hit the spot when you are looking for a healthy but substantial meal at lunchtime. Serve the salad simply on its own or with some whole-wheat bread or whole-grain crackers.

1. Put a skillet over high heat. Add the pumpkin, sunflower, and sesame seeds, cover, and dry-fry for 3–4 minutes, or until lightly toasted and beginning to pop, shaking the pan from time to time. Remove from the heat and stir in the soy sauce.

2. Fill the bottom of a steamer halfway with water, bring to a boil, then put the broccoli into the steamer top. Cover with a lid and steam for 3–5 minutes, or until tender. Transfer to a salad bowl and add the spinach, kale, and cilantro.

3. Put the avocados and half of the lime juice into a small bowl and toss well, then transfer to the salad bowl.

4. To make the dressing, put the remaining lime juice, the oil, honey, and pepper, if using, into a small bowl and whisk together. Sprinkle the toasted seeds over the salad and serve immediately, with the dressing alongside for pouring.

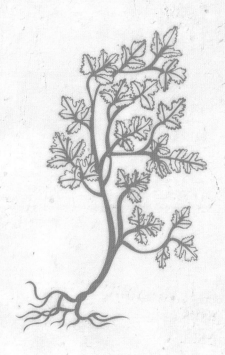

PER SERVING: 343 cal / 28.6g fat / 3.5g sat fat / 20.4g carbs / 5.2g sugar / 8.8g fiber / 8g protein / 360mg sodium

Whole-Wheat Spinach, Pea & Feta Tart

Serves 6

Prep: 35 minutes,
  plus chilling and cooling
Cook: 1–1¼ hours

1 tablespoon unsalted butter
3 scallions, thinly sliced
7 cups baby spinach
⅔ cup shelled peas
3 eggs
1 cup milk
⅓ cup finely crumbled feta cheese
¾ cup cherry tomatoes
salt and pepper, optional

Pastry dough

1 stick unsalted butter, cut into cubes
1¾ cups plus 2 tablespoons
  whole-wheat flour
2 eggs, beaten
1 tablespoon whole-wheat flour,
  for dusting

Great for sharing, this tasty tart is ideal when served either warm or cold, so it can be made ahead and stored in the refrigerator, if you prefer. Serve with a simple side of assorted salad greens for an appetizing meat-free lunch.

1. To make the dough, put the butter and flour into a mixing bowl and season with salt and pepper, if using. Rub the butter into the flour until it resembles fine crumbs. Gradually mix in enough egg to make a soft but not sticky dough.

2. Lightly dust a work surface with whole-wheat flour. Knead the dough gently, then roll it out on the work surface to a little larger than a 10-inch loose-bottom tart pan. Lift the dough over the rolling pin, ease it into the pan, and press it into the sides. Trim the dough so that it stands a little above the top of the pan to allow for shrinkage, then prick the bottom with a fork.

3. Cover the tart shell with plastic wrap and chill in the refrigerator for 15–30 minutes. Meanwhile, preheat the oven to 375°F.

4. To make the filling, melt the butter in a skillet over medium heat. Add the scallions and cook for 2–3 minutes, or until softened. Add the spinach, turn the heat to high, and cook, stirring, until wilted. Set aside to cool.

5. Put the peas into a small saucepan of boiling water and cook for 2 minutes. Drain, then plunge into iced water and drain again. Crack the eggs into a small bowl, add the milk, season with salt and pepper, if using, and beat with a fork.

6. Line the tart shell with a large sheet of parchment paper, add pie weights or dried beans, and place on a baking sheet. Bake for 10 minutes, then remove the paper and weights and bake for an additional 5 minutes, or until the bottom of the tart is crisp and dry.

7. Drain any cooking juices from the scallions and spinach into the eggs. Put the onion mixture into the tart shell, add the peas, then sprinkle with the cheese. Whisk the eggs and milk together once again, then pour into the tart shell and dot the tomatoes over the top. Bake for 40–50 minutes, or until set and golden. Let cool for 20 minutes, then serve.

PER SERVING: *439 cal / 27.1g fat / 15.6g sat fat / 35.9g carbs / 4.9g sugar / 6.2g fiber / 16.4g protein / 280mg sodium*

Fresh Pho with Beef

Transport your taste buds across the world and enjoy the enticing fresh and clean flavors of this wonderful Vietnamese beef and noodle dish—it is a good choice for a flavor-packed lunch with friends.

Serves 4

Prep: 20–25 minutes
Cook: 40 minutes

8½ cups beef broth
1½-inch piece fresh ginger, sliced
1 star anise
2 cinnamon sticks
5 cloves
⅓ cup Thai fish sauce
1 red chile, finely sliced
7 ounces rice vermicelli noodles
12 ounces top sirloin or tenderloin steak, finely sliced
1 cup finely sliced snow peas
½ cup bean sprouts
⅔ cup coarsely chopped fresh cilantro, to garnish
¾ cup coarsely chopped fresh Thai basil, to garnish
1 tablespoon finely sliced red chile, to garnish

1. Pour the beef broth into a large saucepan. Add the ginger, star anise, cinnamon sticks, cloves, fish sauce, and chile to the saucepan and put the pan over high heat. Bring the broth to a boil, then reduce the heat and simmer over low heat, keeping the pan covered with a lid, for 30 minutes.

2. Meanwhile, put the dry noodles into a large bowl, pour boiling water over the top, and let cook for 3–4 minutes, or prepare according to the package directions, until they are completely softened. Drain, return to the bowl, cover, and set aside.

3. Add the steak strips to the beef broth and poach for 2–3 minutes. Remove the ginger slices, star anise, cinnamon sticks, and cloves from the broth with a slotted spoon.

4. Divide the noodles among four deep bowls. Add a handful of raw snow peas and bean sprouts to each, then ladle the hot broth mixture over the noodles. Garnish with the cilantro, Thai basil, and sliced red chile and serve immediately.

PER SERVING: 366 cal / 8.1g fat / 3.3g sat fat / 49.8g carbs / 4.1g sugar / 2.2g fiber / 24.3g protein / 4040mg sodium

Chilled Fava Bean Soup

Serves 6

Prep: 30 minutes,
  plus cooling and chilling
Cook: 12 minutes

3½ cups vegetable broth

4⅓ cups shelled fresh young fava beans

3 tablespoons lemon juice

2 tablespoons chopped
  fresh summer savory

salt and pepper, optional

6 tablespoons Greek-style plain yogurt,
  to serve

1 teaspoon chopped fresh mint,
  to garnish

Gloriously green, this seasonal chilled summer soup showcases fresh young fava beans when they are at their best.

1. Pour the broth into a large saucepan and bring to a boil. Reduce the heat to a simmer, add the fava beans, and cook for about 7 minutes, or until the beans are tender.

2. Remove the pan from the heat and let cool slightly. Transfer to a food processor or blender, in batches if necessary, and process until smooth. Push the mixture through a strainer set over a bowl.

3. Stir in the lemon juice and summer savory and season with salt and pepper, if using. Let cool completely, then cover with plastic wrap and chill in the refrigerator for at least 3 hours.

4. To serve, ladle into chilled bowls or glasses, top each with a tablespoon of yogurt, and garnish with mint. Serve immediately.

PER SERVING: *129 cal / 2.4g fat / 1.2g sat fat / 14.2g carbs / 2.4g sugar / 7.6g fiber / 10.3g protein / 560mg sodium*

Three Bean & Chia Salad

Serves 4
Prep: 20 minutes
Cook: 9 minutes

2 cups halved green beans

1⅓ cups frozen edamame (soybeans)

1 cup frozen corn kernels

1 (15-ounce) can red kidney beans, drained and rinsed

2 tablespoons chia seeds

Dressing

3 tablespoons olive oil

1 tablespoon red wine vinegar

1 teaspoon whole-grain mustard

1 teaspoon agave syrup

4 teaspoons finely chopped fresh tarragon

salt and pepper, optional

Choice chia seeds and protein-providing mixed beans add fiber, vitamins, and minerals to this supersalad, all tossed together in a piquant mustard-tarragon dressing to produce a palate-pleasing energy-boosting lunch.

1. Put the green beans, edamame, and corn kernels into a saucepan of boiling water. Bring back to a boil, then simmer for 4 minutes, or until the green beans are just tender. Drain into a colander, rinse with cold water, then drain again and put into a salad bowl.

2. Add the kidney beans and chia seeds to the bowl and toss gently together.

3. To make the dressing, put the oil, vinegar, and mustard into a screw-top jar, then add the agave syrup and tarragon and season with salt and pepper, if using. Screw on the lid and shake well. Drizzle the dressing over the salad, toss gently together, and serve immediately.

PER SERVING: *302 cal / 15.6g fat / 2g sat fat / 24.4g carbs / 4.5g sugar / 11.1g fiber / 13.4g protein / trace sodium*

Sea Bass & Trout Ceviche

Natural, clean flavors come to the fore in this refreshing combination of fresh fish, fruit, and vegetables to create the ultimate raw food feast. This is perfect for a nourishing meat-free lunch that is low in fat.

Serves 4

Prep: 30 minutes, plus chilling
Cook: No cooking

2 ruby grapefruits
7 ounces sea bass fillets, skinned, pin-boned, and cut into cubes
10½ ounces trout fillets, skinned, pin-boned, and cut into cubes
finely grated zest and juice of 2 limes
1 red chile, seeded and finely chopped
½ red onion, finely chopped
1 tablespoon virgin olive oil
⅓ cup finely chopped fresh cilantro
2¼ cups mixed baby spinach, watercress, and arugula salad
salt and pepper, optional

1. Cut the peel and pith away from the grapefruits with a small serrated knife. Hold each one above a bowl and cut between the membranes to release the sections. Squeeze the juice from the membranes into the bowl.

2. Put the sea bass and trout in a ceramic or glass bowl, sprinkle with the lime zest and juice and chile, then add the red onion, grapefruit sections and juice, and oil. Season with salt and pepper, if using, then gently stir so all the fish is evenly coated in the lime juice.

3. Cover and chill in the refrigerator for 1–1½ hours, or until the fish has taken on a cooked appearance. The sea bass should be bright white and the trout should be a paler, even pink.

4. Add the cilantro and stir gently. Arrange the mixed salad greens on four plates and spoon the ceviche on top, then serve immediately.

PER SERVING: 263 cal / 9.7g fat / 1.6g sat fat / 17.8g carbs / 10.1g sugar / 2.9g fiber / 26.7g protein / 80mg sodium

Protein Rice Bowl

Serves 2

Prep: 25 minutes
Cook: 30 minutes

¾ cup brown rice
2 extra-large eggs
2½ cups spinach
4 scallions, finely chopped
1 red chile, seeded and finely sliced
½ ripe avocado, sliced
2 tablespoons roasted peanuts

Vinaigrette

2 tablespoons olive oil
1 teaspoon Dijon mustard
1 tablespoon apple cider vinegar
juice of ½ a lemon

Brown rice adds important fiber and fresh chile supplies some heat to this protein-rich vegetarian lunch for two.

1. Put the rice into a large saucepan and cover with twice the volume of water. Bring to a boil and simmer for 25 minutes, or until the rice is tender and the liquid has nearly all disappeared. Continue to simmer for an additional few minutes if some liquid remains.

2. Meanwhile, cook your eggs. Bring a small saucepan of water to a boil. Carefully add the eggs to the pan and boil for 7 minutes; the whites will be cooked and the yolks should still be slightly soft. Drain and pour cold water over the eggs to stop them from cooking. When cool enough to handle, tap them on the work surface to crack the shells and peel them. Cut the eggs into quarters.

3. Stir the spinach, half of the scallions, and a little red chile into the cooked rice.

4. To make the vinaigrette, whisk together the olive oil, Dijon mustard, cider vinegar, and lemon juice. Pour the dressing over the warm rice and mix to combine.

5. Divide the rice between two bowls and top each with the remaining scallions, avocado, remaining red chile, peanuts, and egg quarters.

PER SERVING: *653 cal / 33.9g fat / 5.9g sat fat / 71.1g carbs / 4g sugar / 8.7g fiber / 19.1g protein / 120mg sodium*

Clams in a Bacon & Leek Broth

Serves 4
Prep: 20–25 minutes
Cook: 20 minutes

3 pounds, 5 ounces clams, scrubbed
1 teaspoon butter
12 bacon strips, coarsely chopped
2 leeks, sliced
1 garlic clove, finely chopped
½ cup brandy
1¼ cups cold water
½ cup light cream
¼ cup finely chopped fresh
   flat-leaf parsley

Natural, fresh clams, bacon, and leeks unite in a flavorful creamy broth to make this special lunch for sharing with family or friends. Fresh whole-grain bread is all you need to complete the meal.

1. Discard any clams with broken shells or any that refuse to close when tapped.

2. Melt the butter in a deep, heavy saucepan over medium heat. Add the bacon and cook, stirring, for 4–5 minutes, or until crisp and golden. Using a slotted spoon, transfer the bacon to a plate lined with paper towels.

3. Put the leeks and garlic into the saucepan and cook, stirring regularly, for 5 minutes, or until softened but not browned.

4. Pour in the brandy and let simmer for a minute to burn off the alcohol (brandy in a hot saucepan can easily be set alight, so be careful). Add the water and stir well. Turn up the heat to medium–high and, when the water starts to boil, toss in the clams. Put on the lid and steam for 5 minutes, or until the clams have opened.

5. Take the saucepan off the heat. Discard any clams that remain closed. Stir in the bacon and cream. Stir in the parsley and serve in bowls, with a large empty bowl to collect the clamshells.

Flatbread Pizza with Zucchini Ribbons

Quinoa flour adds extra nutrients and appeal to these energy-packed homemade flatbread pizzas, topped with vibrant vegetables and drizzled with garlic oil. Delicious served freshly baked and warm from the oven.

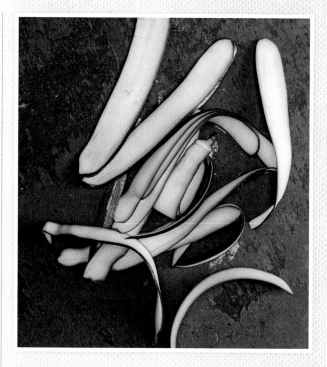

Serves 2

Prep: 30 minutes
Cook: 7–10 minutes

3 tablespoons crème fraîche or sour cream

1 small–medium zucchini, shredded into ribbons, using a vegetable peeler

⅓ cup quartered cherry tomatoes

3 tablespoons ricotta cheese

1 garlic clove, crushed

2 tablespoons olive oil

Pizza crusts

¾ cup whole-wheat flour

⅓ cup plus 1 tablespoon quinoa flour

¾ teaspoon baking soda

1 tablespoon olive oil

2 tablespoons warm water

1 tablespoon whole-wheat flour, for dusting

salt, optional

1. Preheat the oven to 400°F. To make the pizza crusts, put the flours and baking soda into a mixing bowl, season with salt, if using, and stir. Add the oil, then gradually mix in enough of the warm water to make a soft but not sticky dough.

2. Lightly dust a work surface with flour. Knead the dough on the surface for 2 minutes, or until the dough is smooth and slightly elastic.

3. Put two large, flat baking sheets in the oven to get hot.

4. Divide the dough into two pieces. Roll out each piece to a circle about ¼ inch thick. Remove the hot baking sheets from the oven and, working quickly, lay the dough on top. Spread the crème fraîche over the dough, then sprinkle with the zucchini and tomatoes. Spoon small blobs of the ricotta cheese on top.

5. Bake the pizzas for 7–10 minutes, or until the crust is crispy and slightly puffed up, and the ricotta has started to turn golden.

6. Mix the garlic and oil together in a small bowl, and drizzle over the pizzas. Serve immediately.

PER SERVING: *592 cal / 34.4g fat / 10.7g sat fat / 60g carbs / 3.3g sugar / 8.7g fiber / 15.2g protein / 480mg sodium*

Asparagus with Hot-Smoked Salmon & Poached Egg

Serves 2

Prep: 25 minutes, plus chilling
Cook: 26–28 minutes

3½ tablespoons unsalted butter, softened
finely grated zest of ½ lemon
½ teaspoon lemon juice
sprig of fresh dill, coarsely chopped
14 ounces hot-smoked salmon
10 asparagus spears,
   woody stems removed
2 extra-large eggs
salt and pepper, optional

Rich in important omega-3 fatty acids, flakes of hot-smoked salmon are served with antioxidant-rich fresh asparagus spears and good-for-you poached eggs in this scrumptiously satisfying lunch for two to share.

1. Preheat the oven to 350°F. Put the butter, lemon zest and juice, and dill in a small bowl, season with salt and pepper, if using, and mix. Pat the butter into a coarse square with the back of a spoon, wrap it in plastic wrap, and chill in the refrigerator while you make the rest of the dish.

2. Wrap the hot-smoked salmon in aluminum foil and bake in the preheated oven for 15 minutes. Flake the fish into bite-size pieces and keep warm.

3. Cook the asparagus in a small saucepan of boiling water for 2 minutes. Drain and run under a cold running water briefly to stop the cooking process, then set aside.

4. Heat a second wide saucepan of water until it is almost at simmering point. Crack one egg into a cup, then stir the water to make a whirlpool. As the whirlpool slows almost to a stop, gently slip the egg into its center. Cook for 2–3 minutes, then remove with a slotted spoon. Repeat with the second egg.

5. Put five asparagus spears on each of two plates, top with half the flaked salmon, then balance a poached egg on top and crown with half of the lemon butter. The heat from the egg should melt the butter into a scrumptious lemon-herb sauce. Serve immediately.

PER SERVING: *648 cal / 45.6g fat / 19.4g sat fat / 3.9g carbs / 1.8g sugar / 1.8g fiber / 56.2g protein / 3040mg sodium*

Rainbow Nori Rolls

Bright, colorful vegetables, high in antioxidants, provide the nutritious filling for these nourishing sushi-style nori rolls. They are the ideal choice for a special lunch with a small gathering of friends.

Serves 4

Prep: 30–35 minutes, plus cooling and chilling
Cook: 27–30 minutes

1 cup glutinous rice

3 cups cold water

2 tablespoons mirin

1 tablespoon light olive oil

⅔ cup asparagus tips

4 sheets nori

⅓ cup drained, sliced sushi ginger

⅓ cup thin kale strips

1 small red bell pepper, halved, seeded, and cut into thin strips

1 small yellow bell pepper, halved, seeded, and cut into thin strips

2 small carrots, cut into matchstick strips

2 cooked beets in natural juices, drained and cut into matchstick strips

2 tablespoons tamari

2 tablespoons Chinese rice wine

salt, optional

1. Put the rice and water, with a little salt if using, into a saucepan and bring to a boil, stirring occasionally. Reduce the heat and gently simmer for 18–20 minutes, until the rice is soft and has absorbed all the water. Stir occasionally toward the end of cooking so that the rice doesn't stick to the bottom of the pan. Remove from the heat and stir in the mirin. Let cool for 10 minutes.

2. Heat the oil in a skillet, add the asparagus, and sauté over medium heat for 3–4 minutes, until just soft, then set aside.

3. Separate the nori sheets and place one on a piece of plastic wrap set on top of a bamboo sushi mat. Thinly spread one-quarter of the warm rice over the top to cover the nori sheet completely.

4. Arrange one-quarter of the ginger in an overlapping line a little up from one edge of the nori. Arrange one-quarter of the asparagus and kale next to it, then one-quarter of the red and yellow bell peppers, carrots, and beets, leaving a border of rice about ¾ inch wide.

5. Using the plastic wrap and sushi mat, tightly roll the nori around the vegetables. Remove the bamboo mat, then twist the ends of the plastic wrap and place the roll on a tray. Repeat to make three more nori rolls, then chill for 1 hour, or longer if preferred.

6. To serve, mix the tamari and rice wine together, then spoon into four small dipping bowls and set the bowls on serving plates. Unwrap each nori roll and cut into five thick slices. Arrange, cut side up, on the serving plates and serve immediately.

PER SERVING: *280 cal / 4.1g fat / 0.6g sat fat / 50.9g carbs / 7.7g sugar / 5.7g fiber / 6.7g protein / 1360mg sodium*

Turkey Wraps with Avocado Salsa

Wraps are meant for sharing, so these feel-good eats give a great energy boost at lunchtime and are just right for a wholesome weekend of eating al fresco with family or friends. The fun is in the assembling.

Serves 4
Prep: 30 minutes, plus marinating
Cook: 12 minutes

4 thin turkey breast cutlets, about 12 ounces in total
1 tablespoon olive oil, for brushing
4 romaine lettuce leaves, thick stems removed and leaves sliced into ribbons
4 corn tortillas, warmed
3 tablespoons sour cream

Marinade
juice of 2 oranges
1 teaspoon cumin seeds, lightly crushed
½ teaspoon crushed red pepper flakes
¼ cup olive oil
salt and pepper, optional

Salsa
2 avocados, diced
1 small red onion, diced
2 tomatoes, seeded and diced
2 tablespoons chopped fresh cilantro
juice of 1 lime

1. Slice the turkey into 1½ x 2½-inch strips and put into a shallow dish.

2. To make the marinade, whisk together all the marinade ingredients and season with salt and pepper, if using. Pour it over the turkey, cover, and marinate in the refrigerator for at least 4 hours. Remove at least 30 minutes before cooking to bring to room temperature.

3. To make the salsa, mix all the ingredients in a bowl.

4. Preheat the broiler to high. Drain the turkey, discarding the marinade. Thread the strips, accordion-style, onto metal skewers (or use wooden skewers with aluminum foil wrapped around the ends so that they don't burn) and brush with oil. Place the skewers on a rack in the broiler pan and cook under the preheated broiler for about 5 minutes on each side, or until the turkey is cooked all the way through with no pink in the center and starting to brown at the edges. Remove the turkey from the skewers, set aside, and keep warm.

5. Divide the lettuce among the warm tortillas and arrange the turkey on top. Add a little sour cream and salsa. Roll the bottoms and sides of the tortillas over the filling and serve immediately.

PER SERVING: *487 cal / 26g fat / 5g sat fat / 37.2g carbs / 6.2g sugar / 9.6g fiber / 28.5g protein / 240mg sodium*

Spicy Rice with Chicken & Pomegranate

Spice up your lunch with this tempting chicken and rice dish, finished with fleshy pink pomegranate seeds, which pack a powerful nutrient punch, plus vivid green antioxidant-rich fresh herbs.

Serves 4

Prep: 25 minutes, plus cooling
Cook: 45–50 minutes

4 large chicken thighs
2 teaspoons Chinese five spice
2 tablespoons olive oil
2 red onions, finely sliced
2 garlic cloves, finely sliced
5 cardamom pods, crushed
2 star anise
1⅓ cups brown rice
3 cups vegetable broth
½ cup coarsely chopped fresh mint
¼ cup coarsely chopped fresh flat-leaf parsley
seeds of 1 small pomegranate
¼ cup toasted almonds
grated zest and juice of 1 lemon
salt and pepper, optional

1. Preheat the oven to 400°F. Put the chicken thighs onto a baking sheet and sprinkle with the Chinese five spice. Drizzle with 1 tablespoon of olive oil and roast in the preheated oven for 20 minutes, or until the juices run clear when the thickest part of the meat is pierced and no traces of pink remain in the center. Remove from the oven and set aside to cool.

2. Meanwhile, heat the remaining tablespoon of olive oil in a large saucepan over medium–low heat. Add the onion and gently sauté for 10–12 minutes, or until soft and starting to caramelize. Stir in the garlic, cardamom pods, and star anise and cook for an additional minute. Add the rice and stir well.

3. Pour in the broth and bring the pan to a boil. Cover and simmer gently for 25–30 minutes, or until all the broth has been absorbed and the rice is tender.

PER SERVING: *675 cal / 33.9g fat / 7.7g sat fat / 64.2g carbs / 7.8g sugar / 6.2g fiber / 30.3g protein / 880mg sodium*

4. Once the chicken is cool enough to handle, remove the meat from the bones and finely slice. Add to the rice mixture, with any remaining juices, and season with salt and pepper, if using.

5. Stir in half of the mint and parsley. Top with the remaining herbs, pomegranate seeds, toasted almonds, and lemon juice and zest, and serve immediately.

Squash, Chorizo & Goat Cheese Quiche

Why not try your hand at making your own whole-wheat pastry with this fabulous energy-fueled quiche, which can be served either warm or cold? Serve this delicious quiche with a salad of mixed lettuce and peppery arugula.

Serves 4

Prep: 35 minutes, plus chilling and cooling
Cook: 1 hour 20 minutes

3 cups diced butternut squash
1 tablespoon olive oil
7 ounces chorizo, cut into small, irregular chunks
3 eggs
½ cup crème fraîche or Greek-style plain yogurt
2 tablespoons fresh thyme leaves
3½ ounces semi-hard goat cheese
salt and pepper, optional

Pastry dough

3½ tablespoons cold butter, diced
¾ cup whole-wheat flour
2 tablespoons cold water
2 tablespoons whole-wheat flour, for dusting

1. Preheat the oven to 375°F. To make the dough, put the butter into a bowl, add the flour, and season with salt and pepper, if using. Rub the butter into the flour until it resembles bread crumbs. Alternatively, process it in a food processor. Gradually mix in enough of the water to make a soft but not sticky dough.

2. Lightly dust a work surface with flour. Pat the dough into a circle, then wrap it in plastic wrap. Chill in the refrigerator for at least 30 minutes.

3. Meanwhile, to make the filling, put the butternut squash and oil in a large roasting pan, season with salt and pepper, if using, and toss well. Roast in the preheated oven for 15 minutes, then stir and add the chorizo. Roast for an additional 15 minutes, or until the squash is crisp and tender, and the chorizo is crisp. Set aside to cool.

4. Dust the work surface with more flour. Knead the dough gently, then roll out to a circle just under 9 inches in diameter. Place on a baking sheet and prick all over with a fork. Bake for 20 minutes. Remove from the oven and, using the bottom of an 8-inch loose-bottom tart pan as a template, cut a circle in the pastry. Set aside to cool.

5. Meanwhile, crack the eggs into a large bowl and lightly beat with a fork. Stir in the crème fraîche and thyme and season with pepper, if using.

6. Line the 8-inch tart pan with parchment paper. Carefully place your cooled pastry circle in the pan, then sprinkle with the chorizo and butternut squash. Pour over the egg mixture, then crumble the goat cheese on top. Reduce the oven temperature to 325°F. Bake the quiche for 30 minutes, or until the egg in the center is set. Serve warm or cold.

PER SERVING: *724 cal / 54.7g fat / 26.2g sat fat / 34.7g carbs / 3.9g sugar / 5.3g fiber / 26.8g protein / 1000mg sodium*

Seared Beef Salad

Lightly seared succulent tenderloin steaks add an important protein and iron boost to this supersalad, made even more nutritious by the colorful addition of the bright red superfood goji berries.

Serves 4
Prep: 25 minutes
Cook: 6–10 minutes, plus resting

½ iceberg lettuce, leaves separated and torn into bite-size pieces
1¾ cups thinly sliced radishes
4 shallots, thinly sliced
1¼ cups shredded kale
2 tablespoons dried goji berries
½ cup coarsely chopped fresh mint
⅔ cup coarsely chopped fresh cilantro
2 (9-ounce) tenderloin steaks, visible fat removed
¼ cup sunflower oil
juice of 1 lime
1 tablespoon soy sauce
salt and pepper, optional

1. Put the lettuce, radishes, and shallots into a serving bowl. Sprinkle with the kale, goji berries, mint, and cilantro, then toss gently together.

2. Preheat a ridged grill pan over high heat. Brush the steaks with 1 tablespoon of oil, then sprinkle with salt and pepper, if using. Cook in the hot pan for 2 minutes on each side for medium–rare, 3 minutes for medium or 4 minutes for well-done. Transfer the steaks to a plate and let rest for a few minutes.

3. Meanwhile, put the lime juice, soy sauce, and remaining 3 tablespoons of oil into a screw-top jar, screw on the lid, and shake well. Drizzle the dressing over the salad, then toss together.

4. Divide the salad among four bowls. Thinly slice the steak and arrange it over the top, then serve immediately.

PER SERVING: 353 cal / 19.1g fat / 3.2g sat fat / 14.8g carbs / 5.7g sugar / 3.7g fiber / 31.3g protein / 320mg sodium

Shrimp-Filled Baked Sweet Potatoes

Serves 4
Prep: 25 minutes, plus chilling
Cook: 1 hour

4 large sweet potatoes,
    scrubbed and pricked with a fork
½ cup frozen corn kernels
2 plum tomatoes, cut into cubes
4 scallions, finely chopped
1 mango, cut into cubes
¼ cup finely chopped fresh cilantro
1 red chile, seeded and
    finely chopped, optional
10½ ounces cooked
    and peeled shrimp
finely grated zest and juice of 1 lime
1¼ cups low-fat cottage cheese
salt and pepper, optional

Deliciously good for you, adults and children alike will love these zesty sweet potatoes crammed with shrimp and mango salsa.

1. Preheat the oven to 400°F. Put the sweet potatoes on a baking sheet and bake in the preheated oven for 1 hour, or until they feel soft when gently squeezed.

2. Meanwhile, bring a saucepan of water to a boil, add the frozen corn kernels, and cook for 3 minutes, or until tender. Drain into a strainer, then rinse under cold running water.

3. Put the tomatoes, scallions, and mango into a bowl, then stir in the cilantro, red chile, if using, and corn kernels. Season with salt and pepper, if using. Cover and chill in the refrigerator.

4. Put the shrimp and lime zest and juice in another bowl and season with salt and pepper, if using. Cover and chill in the refrigerator.

5. Put the potatoes onto a serving plate, slice them in half, then open them out. Top with spoonfuls of the cottage cheese, then fill with the salsa and shrimp.

PER SERVING: *408 cal / 2.4g fat / 0.7g sat fat / 71.9g carbs / 23.7g sugar / 8g fiber / 24.1g protein / 760mg sodium*

Good-for-You Cobb Salad

As energy levels start to flag, this rich-in-protein layered salad is the perfect choice for those in need of a sustaining and tasty salad at lunchtime. For more mighty appetites, serve with fresh whole-wheat bread alongside.

Serves 2

Prep: 25 minutes
Cook: 50 minutes

Cobb salad

½ cup wild rice
2 extra-large eggs
1 tablespoon olive oil, for frying
2 bacon strips, cut into ¾-inch pieces
1 small avocado, sliced
2 tomatoes, cut into quarters
12 sprigs of watercress
2 tablespoons finely snipped fresh chives, to garnish

Dressing

2 tablespoons apple cider vinegar
1 tablespoon lemon juice
2 teaspoons Dijon mustard
1 garlic clove, crushed
2 tablespoons olive oil

1. To make the Cobb salad, put the wild rice into a small saucepan with 1½ cups of cold water and put over high heat. Bring the pan to a boil and then reduce the heat to low. Simmer the rice for 25 minutes, or until tender. Drain away any excess water and set aside.

2. To make the dressing, put the vinegar, lemon juice, mustard, crushed garlic, and olive oil into a screw-top jar, screw on the lid, and shake well. Or put the ingredients into a small bowl and whisk well until the dressing is thoroughly combined. Set aside.

3. Bring another small saucepan of water to boiling point and gently add the eggs to the pan. Simmer the eggs for 10 minutes. Remove the eggs from the pan and run them under cold water to stop the cooking process. Peel away the eggshells and cut into quarters. Set the egg quarters aside.

PER SERVING: *705 cal / 49.3g fat / 10.2g sat fat / 48.6g carbs / 4g sugar / 9.2g fiber / 20.9g protein / 320mg sodium*

4. Add the olive oil to a small saucepan and put over high heat. Cook the bacon pieces for 4–5 minutes, stirring continuously, or until the bacon is crispy and golden. Set aside.

5. Layer the rice, bacon pieces, avocado, tomatoes, quartered eggs, and watercress between two bowls. Garnish with the chives and drizzle with the dressing. Serve immediately.

Vietnamese Tofu & Noodle Salad

Serves 4

Prep: 30 minutes, plus
    marinating and cooling
Cook: 12 minutes

14 ounces firm chilled tofu,
    drained and cut into 8 slices
4 ounces buckwheat soba noodles
1⅓ cups frozen edamame (soybeans)
1 carrot, cut into matchstick strips
1 cup thin snow pea strips
4 ounces rainbow Swiss chard,
    stems cut into matchstick
    strips, leaves thinly shredded
    (about 2 cups prepared)
¼ cup coarsely chopped fresh cilantro

Marinade

2 tablespoons soy sauce
2 tablespoons sesame seeds
1 red chile, seeded and
    finely chopped, optional
1½-inch piece fresh ginger,
    finely chopped

Dressing

¼ cup virgin canola oil
juice of ½ lemon
1 tablespoon sweet chili dipping sauce

This marvelous meat-free salad combines beneficial buckwheat soba noodles with marinated broiled tofu, nutritious mixed vegetables, and protein-dense edamame (soybeans), all drizzled with a simple chile-spiced salad dressing to serve.

1. Line the bottom of the broiler pan with aluminum foil. Arrange the tofu on the broiler pan in a single layer and fold up the edges of the foil to make a dish.

2. To make the marinade, mix together the soy sauce, sesame seeds, chile, if using, and half of the ginger in a small bowl. Spoon it over the tofu, then let marinate for 10 minutes.

3. Bring a large saucepan of water to a boil, add the noodles and frozen edamame, and cook for 3–4 minutes, or until just tender. Drain into a strainer, then rinse under cold running water.

4. Put the carrot, snow peas, Swiss chard stems and leaves, and cilantro into a large salad bowl. Add the noodles and edamame and gently toss together.

5. To make the dressing, put the oil, lemon juice, sweet chili dipping sauce, and remaining ginger into a bowl and whisk with a fork. Pour it over the salad and gently toss.

6. Preheat the broiler to medium–high. Turn the tofu over in the marinade, then broil for 2 minutes on each side, or until browned. Let cool for a few minutes, then cut into cubes and sprinkle it over the salad with any remaining marinade and serve.

PER SERVING: 412 cal / 22.8g fat / 2.1g sat fat / 33.2g carbs / 6g sugar / 4.9g fiber / 19.9g protein / 840mg sodium

Avocado, Bacon & Chile Frittata

Serves 4
Prep: 20–25 minutes
Cook: 12–16 minutes

1 tablespoon vegetable oil
8 bacon strips, coarsely chopped
6 eggs, beaten
3 tablespoons heavy cream
2 large avocados, sliced
1 red chile, seeded and thinly sliced
½ lime
salt and pepper, optional

Bursting with nourishing nutrients, ripe avocados add appealing flavor, color, and creamy texture to this pan-fried frittata.

1. Preheat the broiler to medium. Heat the oil in an 8-inch ovenproof skillet over medium heat. Add the bacon and cook, stirring, for 4–5 minutes, or until crisp and golden. Using a slotted spoon, transfer to a plate lined with paper towels. Remove the pan from the heat.

2. Pour the eggs into a bowl, add the cream, and season with salt and pepper, if using, then beat. Return the pan to the heat. When it is hot, pour in the egg mixture and cook for 1–2 minutes, without stirring. Sprinkle the bacon and avocado on top and cook for an additional 2–3 minutes, or until the frittata is almost set and the underside is golden brown.

3. Put the frittata under the broiler and cook for 3–4 minutes, or until the top is golden brown and the egg is set. Sprinkle with the chile and squeeze the lime juice over it. Cut into wedges and serve.

PER SERVING: *445 cal / 53.4g fat / 16.6g sat fat / 10.9g carbs / 1.6g sugar / 6.9g fiber / 43.9g protein / 1720mg sodium*

Supercharged
Snacks & Sides

Fig & Oat Bites

The goodness of whole-grain oats paired with fiber-rich dried figs creates these scrumptious nuggets of goodness, which contain no added sugar or salt. A sprinkling of chia seeds and spices boosts their feel-good factor even more.

Makes 25
Prep: 20–25 minutes, plus cooling
Cook: 20 minutes

2¼ cups soft dried figs
3 tablespoons coconut oil, at room temperature
½ teaspoon ground ginger
½ teaspoon ground cinnamon
juice of 1 large orange
2⅓ cups rolled oats
1 tablespoon chia seeds

1. Preheat the oven to 350°F. Line a 9-inch square baking pan with parchment paper.

2. Put the dried figs, coconut oil, ginger, and cinnamon into a food processor and pulse until coarsely chopped. Add the orange juice and oats and pulse again until the mixture just comes together. If a little dry, add a little more orange juice; if a little wet, stir in a few more oats. Add the chia seeds and pulse again briefly.

3. Spoon the dough into the prepared baking pan. Use the back of a greased spatula to push the dough to the corners and spread it evenly.

4. Bake in the preheated oven for 20 minutes. Remove from the oven and, using a sharp knife, cut into 25 small squares. Let cool completely on a wire rack, then serve.

PER SQUARE: *93 cal / 2.4g fat / 1.5g sat fat / 17.5g carbs / 9g sugar / 2.8g fiber / 1.7g protein / trace sodium*

Honey & Spice Snacking Nuts

Serves 6
Prep: 15–20 minutes
Cook: 10 minutes

½ cup Brazil nuts
½ cup pecans
½ cup cashew nuts
3 tablespoons pumpkin seeds
1 tablespoon sunflower oil
1½ tablespoons honey
½ teaspoon ground cinnamon
½ teaspoon ground allspice
½ teaspoon ground black pepper
½ teaspoon sweet paprika
¼ teaspoon salt

Gluten and dairy free, these sensational spiced nuts are quick and easy to make and great for a healthy snack.

1. Line a baking sheet with parchment paper. Preheat the oven to 275°F.

2. Combine all the ingredients in a bowl, except for half a tablespoon of the honey, and then spread out onto the prepared baking sheet.

3. Place onto the middle shelf of the oven and cook for 10 minutes. Remove from the oven and drizzle the remaining honey over the nuts. Let cool, then serve. These snacking nuts can be stored in an airtight container for up to a week.

PER SERVING: *247 cal / 22.3g fat / 3.6g sat fat / 10.5g carbs / 5.5g sugar / 2.5g fiber / 5.4g protein / 80mg sodium*

Roasted Kale Chips

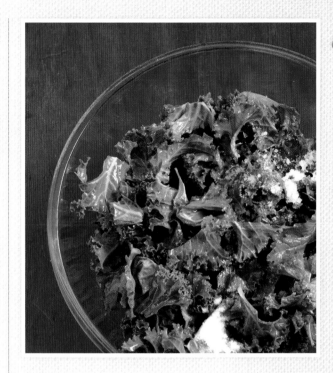

Kale boasts a multitude of nourishing nutrients and these roasted kale chips are perfect for snacking on with a gathering of friends. They make a great alternative to potato chips or tortilla chips.

Serves 4

Prep: 20 minutes
Cook: 10–12 minutes

9 ounces kale
2 tablespoons olive oil
2 pinches of sugar
2 pinches of sea salt
2 tablespoons toasted slivered almonds, to garnish

1. Preheat the oven to 300°F. Remove the thick stems and main rib from the kale (leaving about 2 cups of trimmed leaves). Rinse and dry thoroughly with paper towels. Tear into bite-size pieces and put into a bowl with the oil and sugar, then toss well.

2. Spread about half the leaves in a single layer in a large roasting pan, spaced well apart. Sprinkle with a pinch of sea salt and roast on the bottom rack of the preheated oven for 4 minutes.

3. Stir the leaves, then rotate the baking sheet so the back is at the front. Roast for an additional 1–2 minutes, until the leaves are crisp and slightly browned at the edges. Repeat with the remaining leaves and sea salt. Sprinkle the kale chips with the slivered almonds and serve immediately.

PER SERVING: 122 cal / 9.6g fat / 1.1g sat fat / 8.1g carbs / 1.2g sugar / 1.7g fiber / 3g protein / 160mg sodium

Frozen Yogurt Berries

Serves 4

Prep: 20–25 minutes, plus freezing
Cook: No cooking

1 cup low-fat Greek-style plain yogurt
1 tablespoon honey
¼ teaspoon vanilla extract
¾ cup blueberries
1 cup raspberries

1. Line three baking sheets or pans with nonstick parchment paper, checking first that they will fit into your freezer.

2. Put the yogurt, honey, and vanilla extract in a medium bowl and stir together. Drop a few blueberries into the yogurt, then use two forks to coat the berries in a thin layer of yogurt. Lift out, one berry at a time, draining off the excess yogurt, and transfer to one of the lined baking sheets.

3. Continue dipping and coating until all the blueberries are on the baking sheet. Repeat with the raspberries. Freeze, uncovered, for 2–3 hours, until frozen solid.

4. Lift the berries from the baking sheets and pack into plastic bags or lidded plastic containers. Seal and freeze for up to one month.

5. Remove as many as you need from the freezer and let thaw for 10 minutes before serving so that the fruit can soften slightly.

These berries are perfect for a healthy, quick-fix snack when you've got a sweet craving.

PER SERVING: *81 cal / 0.3g fat / 0g sat fat / 14.5g carbs / 10.8g sugar / 2.7g fiber / 6.4g protein / trace sodium*

Smoky Paprika Roasted Chickpeas

Serves 4

Prep: 15–20 minutes, plus cooling

Cook: 18–24 minutes

2 tablespoons olive oil

1 teaspoon cumin seeds, coarsely crushed

1 teaspoon smoked mild paprika

¼ teaspoon ground allspice

¼ teaspoon ground cinnamon

½ teaspoon sea salt

2 (15-ounce) cans chickpeas in water, drained and rinsed

2 tablespoons date syrup

1. Preheat the oven to 400°F. Add the oil to a roasting pan and place in the oven to heat for 3–4 minutes.

2. Add the cumin seeds, paprika, allspice, cinnamon, and salt to a small bowl and mix together well.

3. Add the chickpeas to the roasting pan, drizzle with the date syrup, sprinkle with the spice mix, and stir together. Roast in the preheated oven for 15–20 minutes, stirring once, until brown and crunchy.

4. Spoon into a bowl and let cool before eating. Store any leftovers in a plastic container or airtight jar in the refrigerator for up to one week.

This is a quick and economical snack to make and perfect for having on the go. For an extra smoky flavor, drizzle with some tahini when adding the date syrup.

PER SERVING: 243 cal / 9.3g fat / 1.2g sat fat / 29.9g carbs / 12.3g sugar / 7.8g fiber / 8.9g protein / 320mg sodium

Date Power Balls

Makes 20

Prep: 30–35 minutes

Cook: No cooking

3 ounces bittersweet chocolate

¼ cup sunflower seeds

¼ cup flaxseed

¼ cup sesame seeds

¾ cup Brazil nuts, coarsely chopped

6 Medjool dates, pitted

⅓ cup goji berries

1 teaspoon ground cinnamon

1 tablespoon maca powder

½ cup dry unsweetened coconut

⅓ cup maple syrup

These fiber-filled, desirable Medjool date power balls are guaranteed to boost your energy levels at any time of the day. They can be made ahead and stored in the refrigerator for a superquick snack.

1. Break 2 ounces of the chocolate into pieces and reserve the rest. Put the sunflower seeds, flaxseed, sesame seeds, Brazil nuts, and chocolate pieces into a food processor and process until finely ground, scraping down the sides of the processor once or twice.

2. Add the dates, goji berries, cinnamon, maca powder, and ⅓ cup of the coconut, then spoon in the maple syrup. Process until you have a coarse paste.

3. Using a measuring spoon, scoop out tablespoons of the mixture onto a plate, then adjust the sizes of the mounds to make 20. Roll them into balls.

4. Put the remaining coconut on one plate and finely grate the remaining chocolate onto another plate. Roll half of the balls in the coconut and the rest in the chocolate. Pack into an airtight container and store in the refrigerator for up to three days.

PER BALL: *253 cal / 9.4g fat / 3.2g sat fat / 15.7g carbs / 9.4g sugar / 3g fiber / 2.9g protein / trace sodium*

Rosemary, Sea Salt & Sesame Popcorn

The perfect power snack, fresh rosemary adds a subtle herb flavor to this sensational seeded popcorn, best enjoyed freshly popped and warm. It's great for snacking on when you want something that isn't sweet but is sustaining.

Serves 4

Prep: 10–15 minutes
Cook: 6–8 minutes

¼ cup sesame seeds
2 tablespoons olive oil
2 rosemary stems, torn into large pieces
¾ cup plus 2 tablespoons popping corn
1 teaspoon sea salt
2 tablespoons balsamic vinegar

1. Add the sesame seeds to a large skillet with 1 teaspoon of the oil. Cover and cook over medium heat for 2–3 minutes, shaking the pan from time to time, until the seeds are toasted golden brown and beginning to pop. Scoop out of the pan into a bowl and wipe out the pan with a piece of paper towel.

2. Add the remaining oil and the rosemary to the pan and heat gently, shaking the pan to release the rosemary's oil. Add the corn, cover with the lid, and cook over medium heat for 3–4 minutes, shaking the pan, until all the popcorn has popped.

3. Remove from the heat, then sprinkle with the toasted sesame seeds and season with the salt and vinegar. Transfer to a serving bowl, discarding the rosemary just before eating.

PER SERVING: 379 cal / 25.2g fat / 3.2g sat fat / 30g carbs / 1.6g sugar / 6.6g fiber / 6.4g protein / 600mg sodium

Butternut Wedges with Sage & Pumpkin Seeds

Serves 3
Prep: 20 minutes
Cook: 35 minutes

1 large butternut squash
1 tablespoon olive oil
½ teaspoon chili powder
12 fresh sage leaves, finely chopped
⅓ cup pumpkin seeds
salt and pepper, optional

1. Preheat the oven to 400°F. Prepare the butternut squash by washing any excess dirt from the skin and slicing off the top and bottom ends.

2. Using a large, sharp knife and a steady hand, cut the squash into six long wedges. Scoop out any seeds and discard. Place the wedges on a baking sheet. Brush with half of the olive oil and sprinkle with the chili powder. Roast in the preheated oven for 25 minutes.

3. Remove from the oven and brush with the remaining olive oil. Sprinkle with the sage and pumpkin seeds. Season with salt and pepper, if using, and return the wedges to the oven for an additional 10 minutes. Serve immediately, garnished with extra pepper, if using.

Once roasted, cut the squash into smaller cubes and toss with toasted couscous for a simple lunch. The edible skin has been kept on in this recipe, but you can peel it off if that is your preference.

PER SERVING: 259 cal / 13.3g fat / 2.1g sat fat / 33.9g carbs / 6.1g sugar / 7.2g fiber / 7.8g protein / trace sodium

Spiced Mashed Carrots

Serves 4

Prep: 20 minutes, plus cooling
Cook: 30–35 minutes

2¾ pounds carrots, cut in half lengthwise
1 small bulb of garlic, cloves peeled
1 teaspoon ground turmeric
1 teaspoon ground coriander
1 teaspoon ground cumin
2 tablespoons olive oil
salt and pepper, optional
2 teaspoons black onion seeds, to garnish
1 tablespoon coarsely chopped fresh
    flat-leaf parsley, to garnish, optional

1. Preheat the oven to 400°F.

2. Put the carrots, garlic cloves, turmeric, coriander, and cumin into a large roasting pan. Drizzle with the olive oil and stir well, until the carrots are coated thoroughly. Season with salt and pepper, if using.

3. Roast in the preheated oven for 30–35 minutes, or until soft. Turn once, about halfway through, to be sure of even cooking.

4. Remove from the oven and let cool slightly. Firmly mash the carrot mixture until you have a soft consistency, adding a touch of hot water, if needed. Season again to taste, if desired.

5. Serve immediately in a warm serving dish, garnished with black onion seeds and parsley, if desired.

This is a versatile side dish, suitable for roasts, tarts, or salads. Try experimenting with other roasted vegetables, such as sweet potatoes or parsnips, for a slightly different variation.

Sweet Potato Falafels

Oven roasting these tasty sesame-coated sweet potato and chickpea falafels instead of frying them helps to keep their fat content down and creates an energy-boosting vegetarian snack, ideal for sharing. Enjoy them either hot or cold.

Makes 16

Prep: 30–35 minutes, plus chilling
Cook: 35–40 minutes

2 sweet potatoes (about 1 ¼ pounds), cut into chunks
1 tablespoon ground cumin
1 teaspoon ground coriander
1 teaspoon ground turmeric
1 tablespoon olive oil, for roasting
1 (15-ounce) can chickpeas, drained and rinsed
¾ cup plus 1 tablespoon chickpea (besan) flour
⅓ cup fresh flat-leaf parsley leaves
½ cup fresh cilantro leaves
1 teaspoon salt
⅔ cup sesame seeds
2 tablespoons olive oil, for drizzling
½ cup plain yogurt, to serve

1. Preheat the oven to 400°F. Put the sweet potato chunks into a roasting pan. Sprinkle with 2 teaspoons of the cumin and all of the ground coriander and turmeric. Pour the olive oil over the sweet potatoes and mix well so the they are coated in the spice paste. Make sure the chunks are spread in an even layer and roast in the preheated oven for 20 minutes.

2. Remove the sweet potatoes from the oven and transfer to a food processor. Add the chickpeas, chickpea flour, parsley, cilantro, salt, and the remaining teaspoon of cumin. Process to a paste. Don't overwork the mixture—stop as soon as you have a paste. Transfer the mixture to a refrigerator and let chill for 15–20 minutes.

PER FALAFEL: *132 cal / 6.6g fat / 1g sat fat / 14.8g carbs / 3g sugar / 3.4g fiber / 3.8g protein / 160mg sodium*

3. Preheat the oven again to 350°F. Shape the cooled chickpea mixture into 16 golf ball-size pieces. Roll each ball in sesame seeds, drizzle with 1 tablespoon of the olive oil, and roast in the preheated oven for 15–20 minutes, turning the falafels over halfway through. At the end of the cooking time, the sesame seeds should be golden.

4. Drizzle the hot falafels with the remaining olive oil and serve with the yogurt. Serve immediately or store in the refrigerator and eat chilled within 24 hours.

Cranberry & Red Cabbage Slaw

Quick and easy to assemble, this colorful slaw is a refreshing combination of raw vegetables and fruit, boosted with dried cranberries, chopped walnuts, and chia seeds, to create a satisfying side for vegetarians and vegans.

Serves 4
Prep: 20 minutes, plus optional chilling
Cook: 2–3 minutes

1½ cups thinly shredded red cabbage
1 carrot, shredded
1 cup cauliflower florets
1 red-skinned sweet, crisp apple, quartered, cored, and thinly sliced
¼ cup dried cranberries
1½ cups alfalfa and sango radish sprouts or alfalfa sprouts

Dressing
½ cup coarsely chopped walnuts
juice of 1 orange
¼ cup virgin olive oil
2 tablespoons chia seeds
salt and pepper, optional

1. Put the red cabbage, carrot, and cauliflower into a salad bowl. Add the apple, dried cranberries, and sprouts and toss well.

2. To make the dressing, put the walnuts into a large skillet and toast for 2–3 minutes, or until just beginning to brown.

3. Put the orange juice, oil, and chia seeds into a small bowl, season with salt and pepper, if using, then stir in the hot walnuts. Pour the dressing over the salad and toss gently. Serve immediately or cover and chill in the refrigerator until needed.

PER SERVING: *315 cal / 23.6g fat / 2.8g sat fat / 25.7g carbs / 15.3g sugar / 6.4g fiber / 4.8g protein / 40mg sodium*

Basil & Lemon Cauliflower Rice

Raw cauliflower is pulsed in a food processor to resemble rice grains, then pan-fried with celery and garlic and combined with basil, lemon, watercress, and hazelnuts to make this intriguing and nutritious side dish.

Serves 4
Prep: 20–25 minutes, plus cooling
Cook: 15–20 minutes

¾ cup skin-on hazelnuts, coarsely chopped
1 small head of cauliflower
1 tablespoon olive oil
2 celery stalks, coarsely chopped
3 garlic cloves, coarsely chopped
¾ cup coarsely chopped fresh basil
zest and juice of 1 lemon
2 cups chopped watercress or other peppery greens
salt and pepper, optional

1. Add the chopped hazelnuts to a large, dry skillet. Toast over medium heat until golden. Remove the hazelnuts from the pan and set aside.

2. Remove the core from the cauliflower and divide the florets. Put into a food processor and pulse until the cauliflower resembles rice grains. Put into a bowl and set aside.

3. Pour the olive oil into a skillet over medium heat and sauté the celery and garlic for 5–6 minutes, or until soft.

4. Add the cauliflower rice to the skillet and stir to combine. Cook, stirring occasionally, for 8–10 minutes. Remove from the heat and let the mixture cool for a few minutes before adding the basil, lemon zest, lemon juice, toasted hazelnuts, and watercress. Season with salt and pepper, if using, and serve immediately.

PER SERVING: *182 cal / 14.4g fat / 1.3g sat fat / 11.4g carbs / 3.7g sugar / 4.7g fiber / 5.7g protein / 40mg sodium*

Orzo with Mint & Fresh Tomatoes

Serves 4
Prep: 20 minutes
Cook: 20 minutes

2 cups orzo
½ cup crème fraîche or sour cream
5½ cups baby spinach
½ cup coarsely chopped fresh mint
16 cherry tomatoes, coarsely chopped
salt and pepper, optional
1 tablespoon coarsely chopped fresh mint, to garnish

Orzo pasta, which resembles fat grains of rice, pairs up with baby spinach and cherry tomatoes in this delightful salad finished with chopped mint leaves, making it the perfect palate-pleasing and fresh-tasting meat-free side.

1. Bring a large saucepan of water to a boil and drop the orzo into the water. Stir vigorously to prevent the little grains from sticking and then stir occasionally during cooking. Simmer for 8 minutes, or according to the package directions until the orzo is tender but still firm to the bite. Scoop out ½ cup of the cooking water and set aside.

2. Drain the orzo and return to the pan with the reserved cooking water. Put the pan over gentle heat and add the crème fraîche and spinach. Stir until the spinach has wilted and the crème fraîche has coated the grains. Remove from the heat.

3. Stir in the mint and cherry tomatoes. Season with salt and pepper, if using.

4. Garnish with mint and serve immediately.

PER SERVING: *443 cal / 11.4g fat / 7.1g sat fat / 70.9g carbs / 5.1g sugar / 5g fiber / 14g protein / 40mg sodium*

Baby Broccoli with Pine Nuts

Serves 4
Prep: 25 minutes
Cook: 20–25 minutes

1½ pounds baby broccoli
3 tablespoons extra virgin olive oil
3 shallots, thinly sliced
2 large garlic cloves, thinly sliced
pinch of crushed red pepper flakes
3 tablespoons pine nuts, toasted
4 tablespoons butter
2 tablespoons capers, drained
¼ cup snipped fresh chives
¼ cup Parmesan cheese shavings
salt and pepper, optional

A well-renowned superfood, baby broccoli forms the basis of this nutrient-busting, gluten-free side dish. High in healthy unsaturated fats, the toasted pine nuts add plenty of extra flavor and crunch, too.

1. Cut off the broccoli florets and slice lengthwise if thick. Slice the leaves and stems into ¾-inch pieces. Steam for 2 minutes over a saucepan of boiling water, until barely soft. Remove from the heat. Reserve the cooking water.

2. Heat the oil in a large skillet over medium–low heat. Add the shallots and sauté for 5 minutes.

3. Add the garlic and sauté for 2–3 minutes, or until just starting to brown.

4. Increase the heat to medium and add the broccoli to the pan. Add the crushed red pepper flakes and season with salt and pepper, if using. Add 3–4 tablespoons of the broccoli cooking water. Cook and keep stirring for 4–6 minutes, or until the broccoli is just tender and the color is still bright green.

5. Stir in the pine nuts and check the seasoning. Transfer to a serving dish and keep warm.

6. Heat a heavy skillet. When it is hot, add the butter and sizzle until golden.

7. Remove from the heat and stir in the capers and half of the chives.

8. Pour the sauce over the broccoli. Sprinkle with the cheese shavings and the remaining chives.

PER SERVING: 331 cal / 28g fat / 9.9g sat fat / 16.1g carbs / 3.8g sugar / 5.3g fiber / 8.8g protein / 400mg sodium

Brown Rice with Pistachio Nuts, Parsley & Dried Cherries

Serves 4

Prep: 20 minutes, plus cooling
Cook: 30–35 minutes

2 cups brown rice
4 cups vegetable broth
⅔ cup dried cherries
1 small red onion, finely chopped
2 garlic cloves, crushed
¼ cup coarsely chopped fresh parsley
2 tablespoons olive oil
¾ cup chopped pistachio nuts
salt and pepper, optional
2 tablespoons coarsely chopped
   fresh parsley, to garnish

Full-of-fiber cooked brown rice is tossed with dried cherries and red onion, then finished with fresh parsley and chopped pistachios to create this energy-giving side that is suitable for vegetarians and vegans alike.

1. Put the rice into a large saucepan and cover well with the vegetable broth. Bring to a simmer and cook for 25 minutes, or according to the package directions, until the rice is tender and nearly all of the broth has disappeared. Continue to simmer for an additional few minutes if some broth remains.

2. Transfer the cooked rice to a large bowl and stir in the dried cherries, red onion, and garlic. Season with salt and pepper, if using.

3. Let the rice mixture cool for a few minutes before adding the chopped parsley, olive oil, and half of the pistachio nuts. Stir thoroughly until well combined.

4. Pile the warm rice mixture onto a serving dish and garnish with the remaining chopped pistachio nuts and the chopped parsley. Serve immediately.

PER SERVING: 684 cal / 22.9g fat / 3.9g sat fat / 108.1g carbs / 17.6g sugar / 7.7g fiber / 14.8g protein / 960mg sodium

Steamed Greens with Lemon & Cilantro

Serves 4
Prep: 15 minutes
Cook: 6 minutes

*1 small head of cabbage (about 1 pound),
tough outer leaves discarded*

7 cups baby spinach

large pat of unsalted butter

finely grated zest of ½ lemon

¼ cup chopped fresh cilantro

salt and pepper, optional

This nutritious mix of lightly steamed greens tossed with butter, lemon zest, and cilantro is quick and easy to make.

1. Cut the cabbage into quarters lengthwise and cut out the tough core. Slice the quarters crosswise into ¾-inch ribbons. Steam for 3 minutes, or until starting to soften.

2. Arrange the spinach on top of the cabbage and steam for an additional 3 minutes. Drain in a colander to remove any excess liquid.

3. Transfer the cabbage and spinach to a warm serving dish. Stir in the butter, lemon zest, and cilantro, mixing well.

4. Season with salt and pepper, if using, and serve immediately.

PER SERVING: *63 cal / 3.4g fat / 2g sat fat / 7.4g carbs / 4.2g sugar / 3.5g fiber / 2.7g protein / 40mg sodium*

Dressings,
Sauces & Dips

Ginger, Garlic & Soy Dressing

Widely regarded for its anti-inflammatory properties, fresh ginger adds a wonderful aromatic, spicy flavor to this Chinese-style dressing. For those who follow a gluten-free diet, be sure to use tamari or a gluten-free soy sauce.

Makes ⅔ cup
Prep: 10 minutes, plus chilling
Cook: No cooking

2¼-inch piece of ginger, grated, juices reserved
2 garlic cloves, crushed
2 tablespoons rice vinegar
2 tablespoons dark soy sauce
1 teaspoon superfine sugar
3 tablespoons olive oil
2 tablespoons water

1. Put the ginger into a screw-top jar with any juices. Add the garlic, rice vinegar, soy sauce, superfine sugar, olive oil, and water. Shake well until thoroughly combined.

2. Chill and store in the refrigerator until ready to use. This dressing improves with age, so prepare the day before it is needed, if possible. This dressing goes well with a Chinese noodle salad or chopped Chinese greens.

PER ⅔ CUP: *400 cal / 40.5g fat / 5.6g sat fat / 8.6g carbs / 4.8g sugar / 0.4g fiber / 2.4g protein / 1800mg sodium*

Tahini & Lemon Dressing

Tahini, or sesame seed paste, is full of essential nutrients, including healthy unsaturated fats and fiber. Combined with freshly squeezed lemon juice and flavored with paprika and garlic, it forms a flavorful salad dressing.

Makes 1¼ cups

Prep: 10 minutes
Cook: No cooking

⅓ cup tahini
juice of 2 lemons (about ⅔ cup)
¼ cup water
¼ teaspoon paprika
1 garlic clove, crushed
pinch of salt

1. Put all of the ingredients into a food processor or blender and process until smooth. Add more paprika to taste, if desired.

2. If making by hand, thoroughly whisk together the tahini, lemon juice, water, paprika, garlic, and salt in a bowl. You're aiming for a creamy, smooth texture. If it's too thick, add more water.

3. Serve immediately or place in a covered container in the refrigerator. This will keep in the refrigerator for up to three days. This dressing goes well with Greek salad.

PER 1¼ CUPS: 634 cal / 54.3g fat / 7.6g sat fat / 32.8g carbs / 4.4g sugar / 10g fiber / 17.8g protein / 720mg sodium

Avocado, Lemon & Paprika Dressing

Makes 1¼ cups

Prep: 15 minutes

Cook: No cooking

1 ripe avocado, coarsely chopped

juice of a large lemon

1 small garlic clove

½ teaspoon paprika

⅓–½ cup cold water

1. Put the avocado, lemon juice, garlic, and paprika into a blender or food processor. Process until the mixture is well blended.

2. Slowly add the water until you reach the desired consistency. Pour the dressing into a small bowl and use as required.

3. This dressing can be made up to 3–4 hours in advance. Serve immediately or put into a covered container in the refrigerator for up to 1 day. This dressing goes well with salad or as a dip for chopped vegetables.

This flavor combination works really well together and could be a wonderful dip to serve with root vegetable fries. Simply remove the cold water from the recipe.

PER 1¼ CUPS: *342 cal / 29.8g fat / 4.3g sat fat / 22.5g carbs / 3g sugar / 14.1g fiber / 4.5g protein / trace sodium*

Garlic & Jalapeño Dipping Oil

Makes about 1 cup

Prep: 15 minutes, plus cooling

Cook: 1½–2 hours

5 garlic cloves, halved lengthwise

2 tablespoons seeded and chopped jalapeño chile

1 teaspoon dried oregano

1 cup canola oil

1. Preheat the oven to 300°F. Combine the garlic, chile, and oregano with the oil in a small ovenproof dish.

2. Place the dish on a pie plate in the center of the preheated oven for 1½–2 hours. The temperature of the oil should reach 250°F.

3. Using thick oven mitts, carefully remove the small dish from the oven, let cool, then strain through cheesecloth into a clean jar.

4. Store in an airtight container in the refrigerator for up to one month. You can also leave the garlic and chile pieces in the oil and strain before using.

Be especially careful during the heating of the oil stage in this recipe.

PER 1 CUP: *1989 cal / 225g fat / 16.6g sat fat / 0g carbs / 0g sugar / 0g fiber / 0g protein / trace sodium*

Lime & Miso Dressing

Makes 2/3 cup
Prep: 10 minutes, plus chilling
Cook: No cooking

1 tablespoon Thai fish sauce
1 tablespoon rice vinegar
1 tablespoon miso paste
grated zest and juice of 2 limes
2 tablespoons sesame oil
2 teaspoons white sesame seeds
salt and pepper, optional

1. Put the fish sauce, rice vinegar, miso paste, lime juice, and sesame oil into a screw-top jar. Add the lime zest and season with salt and pepper, if using.

2. Seal the jar and shake to mix thoroughly. Stir in the sesame seeds.

3. Chill in the refrigerator until ready to use. Drizzle the dressing over salads to serve.

This dressing could also be used as a great dipping sauce for dim sum or sushi.

PER 2/3 CUP: 356 cal / 31.5g fat / 4.5g sat fat / 15.9g carbs / 3.7g sugar / 2.6g fiber / 5g protein / 2320mg sodium

Wasabi & Soy Dressing

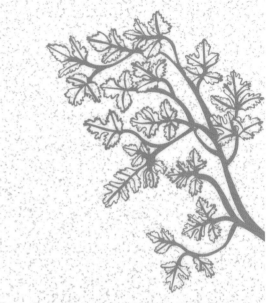

Makes ⅓ cup
Prep: 10 minutes
Cook: No cooking

3 tablespoons peanut oil
juice of ½ lime
1 teaspoon wasabi paste
1 tablespoon soy sauce
1 teaspoon sesame oil
½ teaspoon packed dark brown sugar
1 tablespoon rice wine vinegar

1. Put all of the ingredients into a small bowl. Whisk the mixture together with a fork until all of the sugar has dissolved.

2. Serve the dressing immediately to drizzle over salads. This dressing goes particularly well with plain salads that need pepping up with some heat.

For extra zing, add the finely grated zest of a lemon to the dressing.

PER ⅓ CUP: 437 cal / 45g fat / 7.4g sat fat / 8.4g carbs / 4g sugar / 0.2g fiber / 1.1g protein / 1040mg sodium

Caper & Oregano Vinaigrette

Extra virgin olive oil, which is naturally high in healthy monounsaturated fat and low in saturated fat, is the top oil to pick for this herb-packed vinaigrette. Capers add extra distinctive flavor and appeal, too.

Makes ½ cup
Prep: 15 minutes
Cook: No cooking

juice of 2 lemons
1 tablespoon finely chopped capers
2 tablespoons finely chopped fresh oregano
2 garlic cloves, crushed
¼ cup extra virgin olive oil
pinch of brown sugar
salt and pepper, optional

1. Simply squeeze the lemon juice into a small bowl and stir in the capers, oregano, garlic, olive oil, and brown sugar. Whisk well and season with salt and pepper, if using.

2. Serve immediately or place in a covered container and keep in the refrigerator for up to one month. This goes well with any salad or drizzled over mozzarella cheese.

PER ½ CUP: 519 cal / 54.4g fat / 7.5g sat fat / 11.6g carbs / 3.8g sugar / 1.5g fiber / 1.1g protein / 240mg sodium

Healthy Caesar Dressing

Low-fat plain yogurt and reduced-fat mayo combine to provide the perfect basis for this lighter, healthy alternative to Caesar dressing, which is filled with flavor from the anchovies, garlic, lemon, and parsley.

Makes ½ cup
Prep: 15 minutes
Cook: No cooking

½ cup low-fat Greek-style plain yogurt

3 anchovy fillets, coarsely chopped

2 garlic cloves, crushed

grated zest and juice from ½ lemon

⅓ cup coarsely chopped fresh flat-leaf parsley

1 tablespoon low-fat mayonnaise

1. Put all of the ingredients, except the mayonnaise, into a small bowl and pulse with a handheld blender until the parsley and anchovies have disintegrated. As the parsley breaks down, the dressing will take on a beautiful green color and become easier to blend.

2. Stir in the mayonnaise. Serve immediately as an alternative to Caesar dressing. This will also keep for three to four days in a covered container in the refrigerator.

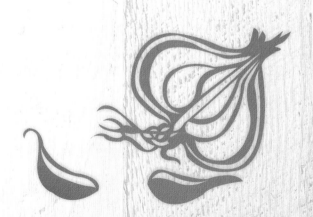

PER ½ CUP: *147 cal / 5.3g fat / 0.7g sat fat / 10.6g carbs / 5g sugar / 1.2g fiber / 15g protein / 600mg sodium*

Slow-Cooked Tomato Pasta Sauce

Makes 3 cups
Prep: 20 minutes, plus cooling
Cook: 1 hour 40 minutes

¼ cup olive oil

1 onion, chopped

5 garlic cloves, finely sliced

2 tablespoons coarsely chopped fresh flat-leaf parsley

2 tablespoons coarsely chopped fresh basil

13 tomatoes (about 3¼ pounds), cored and coarsely chopped

1 teaspoon firmly packed light brown sugar

1 tablespoon red wine vinegar

salt and pepper, optional

1. Heat the olive oil in a heavy saucepan over medium heat. Add the onion and sauté gently until it softens and turns almost golden.

2. Add the garlic and herbs and sauté for 30 seconds before carefully adding the chopped tomatoes, including the seeds and skin. Stir in the sugar and vinegar. Season with salt and pepper, if using, then reduce the heat to medium–low and simmer the sauce, uncovered, for 1½ hours, or until the tomatoes have broken down and the sauce has thickened. Stir occasionally to prevent anything from catching on the bottom of the pan. At the end, season again with salt and pepper, if using.

3. Let cool slightly and serve mixed into pasta or spaghetti, or as required. If you like your sauce to be a little smoother, simply blend using a food processor or handheld blender.

Once made, this sauce can be divided into containers and frozen for up to three months.

PER 3 CUPS: 805 cal / 53.3g fat / 7.3g sat fat / 79.2g carbs / 49.3g sugar / 20.6g fiber / 15.7g protein / 80mg sodium

Avocado & Cashew Nut Pasta Sauce

Makes 1¾ cups
Prep: 20 minutes
Cook: 3–4 minutes

1 cup cashew nuts
2 garlic cloves, chopped
⅔ cup fresh mint leaves
2 perfectly ripe avocados, coarsely chopped
½ cup plus 1 tablespoon finely grated Parmesan cheese
2 tablespoons olive oil
juice of 1 lime
1–2 tablespoons water

1. Toast the cashews in a dry skillet over high heat for 3–4 minutes, moving the pan regularly to prevent the nuts from burning.

2. Put the cashew nuts and garlic cloves into a food processor and pulse until the nuts are finely chopped. Add the mint leaves, avocados, and Parmesan cheese. Blend, and with the motor running, pour in the olive oil and lime juice. Add just enough water to reach a thick sauce consistency.

3. Use immediately or keep in the refrigerator in a covered container. The sauce will keep for up to two days. Serve mixed into pasta.

This recipe relies on perfectly ripe avocados—to ripen a hard avocado, put it into a paper bag with a banana or an apple overnight.

PER 1¾ CUPS: *1666 cal / 142.9g fat / 28.4g sat fat / 74.1g carbs / 9.8g sugar / 32.6g fiber / 45.7g protein / 800mg sodium*

Beet & Hazelnut Pesto

Serves 8

Prep: 20–25 minutes, plus cooling

Cook: 1 hour

4 raw beets
½ cup extra virgin olive oil
1 cup roasted hazelnuts
2 garlic cloves, peeled
1⅓ cups freshly grated fresh Parmesan cheese
salt and pepper, optional

1. Preheat the oven to 350°F.

2. Sprinkle the beets with a little salt and pepper, if using, then drizzle with a small amount of the olive oil. Wrap the beets in aluminum foil and put into the oven. Cook for 1 hour. To test if the beets are cooked, check with the tip of a small, sharp knife; the blade should go in with ease.

3. Remove the cooked beets from the oven and let cool. Once cool, peel away the skin and discard.

4. Put the hazelnuts and garlic into a food processor and process for 30 seconds.

5. Add the beets and salt and pepper, if using, and process again, adding the remaining olive oil, a little at a time, through the feeder tube, until combined.

6. Transfer the pesto to a medium bowl and mix in the Parmesan cheese.

7. This pesto can be served with vegetable sticks or mixed into pasta or spaghetti.

This is a great alternative to basil pesto, adding nutrients with the beets and nuts.

PER SERVING: 274 cal / 25.2g fat / 4.7g sat fat / 6.2g carbs / 2.9g sugar / 2.2g fiber / 7.8g protein / 240mg sodium

Beet & Cucumber Tzatziki on Salad Greens

Serves 4

Prep: 20 minutes
Cook: No cooking

2 cooked beets in natural juices, drained and diced
1 cup diced cucumber
⅓ cup diced radishes
1 scallion, finely chopped
12 small butterhead lettuce leaves

Dressing

⅔ cup low-fat Greek-style plain yogurt
¼ teaspoon ground cumin
½ teaspoon honey
2 tablespoons finely chopped fresh mint
salt and pepper, optional

1. To make the dressing, put the yogurt, cumin, and honey into a bowl. Stir in the mint and season with salt and pepper, if using.

2. Add the beets, cucumber, radishes, and scallion, then toss gently together.

3. Arrange the lettuce leaves on a plate. Spoon a little of the tzatziki into each leaf. Serve immediately.

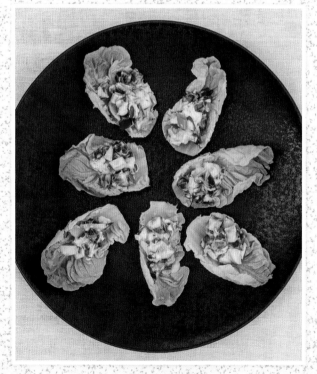

These are perfect for serving as canapés or as a sharing snack with friends.

PER SERVING: 51 cal / 0.2g fat / 0g sat fat / 8.2g carbs / 5.7g sugar / 1.8g fiber / 5.1g protein / 40mg sodium

Guacamole Dip

Crammed with creamy avocado flesh, this popular dip is also jam-packed with nutrients, including heart-friendly monounsaturated fat and vitamin C, plus it can be enjoyed by people with allergies and vegans too.

Serves 4

Prep: 15 minutes
Cook: No cooking

2 large avocados, sliced
juice of 2 limes
2 large garlic cloves, crushed
1 teaspoon mild chili powder
salt and pepper, optional
1 teaspoon mild chili powder, to garnish

1. Put the avocado slices, lime juice, garlic, and chili powder into a food processor and process until smooth. Season with salt and pepper, if using.

2. Transfer to a serving bowl, garnish with chili powder, and serve immediately.

Baba Ghanoush

Serves 6
Prep: 20 minutes, plus cooling
Cook: 1 hour

2 extra-large eggplants
1 garlic clove, chopped
2 teaspoons ground cumin
¼ cup tahini
2 tablespoons lemon juice
¼ cup plain yogurt
2 tablespoons chopped fresh cilantro
1 tablespoon chopped fresh cilantro, to garnish

1. Preheat the oven to 425°F. Prick the eggplant skins and put them onto a baking sheet. Bake in the preheated oven for 1 hour, or until soft. Remove from the oven and set aside to cool.

2. Peel off and discard the eggplant skins. Coarsely chop the flesh and put it into a food processor. Add the garlic, cumin, tahini, lemon juice, yogurt, and cilantro and process until smooth and combined, scraping down the sides as necessary.

3. Transfer to a serving dish, garnish with a little cilantro, and serve. If you are preparing this ahead of serving, cover the dish tightly with plastic wrap and store in the refrigerator until 30 minutes before serving.

This dip is a classic Middle Eastern mezze dish and tastes great when served with pita bread.

PER SERVING: 107 cal / 6.1g fat / 1g sat fat / 12.2g carbs / 4.3g sugar / 6.3g fiber / 3.8g protein / trace sodium

Basil & Raw Garlic Hummus

Serves 4
Prep: 15–20 minutes
Cook: No cooking

1 (15-ounce) can chickpeas, drained and rinsed
3 tablespoons tahini
¾ cup coarsely chopped fresh basil
pinch of paprika
2 garlic cloves
finely grated zest and juice of 1 lemon
¼–⅓ cup cold water
salt and pepper, optional
1 cup fresh basil sprigs, to garnish

1. Put the chickpeas, tahini, basil, paprika, garlic cloves, and lemon zest and juice into a food processor. Process to a coarse mixture.

2. With the food processor still running, slowly add the cold water until a smooth, thick paste is formed, adding a little more, if needed. Season with salt and pepper, if using.

3. Garnish with basil and serve immediately or put into a covered container and keep in the refrigerator. This will keep in the refrigerator for up to three days.

Hummus can have so many different variations, so once you have the staple chickpea, tahini, and garlic version under your belt, try adding different flavors; harissa or olives work well.

PER SERVING: *152 cal / 7.3g fat / 1g sat fat / 15g carbs / 3.4g sugar / 5.3g fiber / 6.4g protein / trace sodium*

Fava Bean & Mint Hummus with Vegetable Sticks

Serves 4
Prep: 30–35 minutes
Cook: 15 minutes

2⅓ cups shelled fava beans
2 tablespoons virgin olive oil
1 teaspoon cumin seeds, crushed
3 scallions, thinly sliced
2 garlic cloves, finely chopped
½ cup torn fresh mint pieces
¼ cup finely chopped fresh
    flat-leaf parsley
juice of 1 lemon
¼ cup Greek-style plain yogurt
salt and pepper, optional

To serve

1 red and 1 yellow bell pepper,
    seeded and cut into sticks
4 celery stalks, cut into sticks
½ cucumber, halved, seeded
    and cut into sticks
4 pita breads, cut into strips, optional

Fava beans are an excellent vegetable source of protein and fiber, so when combined with fresh garden herbs and garlic, they make a great-tasting healthy hummus that is just right served with colorful, raw vegetable sticks.

1. Fill the bottom of a steamer halfway with water. Bring the steamer to a boil, then put the fava beans into the steamer top. Cover with a lid and steam for 10 minutes, or until tender.

2. Meanwhile, heat the oil in a skillet over medium heat. Add the cumin, scallions, and garlic, and cook for 2 minutes, or until the scallions are softened.

3. Put the beans into a food processor or blender, add the scallion mixture, herbs, lemon juice, and yogurt, and season with salt and pepper, if using. Process to a coarse puree, then spoon into a dish set on a large plate.

4. Arrange the vegetable sticks around the hummus and serve with the pitas, if using.

PER SERVING: *202 cal / 8.6g fat / 1.5g sat fat / 17.3g carbs / 4.6g sugar / 8.1g fiber / 9.8g protein / 40mg sodium*

A Feast
of Vegetables

Mushrooms & Squash on Buckwheat

Serves 4
Prep: 25 minutes
Cook: 40–45 minutes

2¼-pounds squash, such as
   Crown Prince or Kabocha
1 tablespoon thick balsamic vinegar
½ cup olive oil
large pat of butter
1⅓ cups roasted buckwheat, rinsed
1 egg, lightly beaten
2 cups vegetable broth
1 onion, halved and sliced
4 cups quartered small
   cremini mushrooms
2 tablespoons lemon juice
⅓ cup chopped fresh flat-leaf parsley
¼ cup coarsely chopped walnuts
salt and pepper, optional

Buckwheat is naturally gluten-free and provides a balanced base for this tempting vegetable dish. Roasted squash adds important antioxidants, while walnuts add crunch and health-benefiting omega-3 fatty acids.

1. Preheat the oven to 400°F. Cut the squash into eight wedges, peel, and seed.

2. Put the squash into a roasting pan and toss with the vinegar and ⅓ cup of the oil. Season with salt and pepper, if using, and dot with the butter. Roast in the preheated oven for 25–30 minutes, until slightly caramelized.

3. Meanwhile, put the buckwheat into a large skillet. Add the egg, stirring to coat the grains. Stir over medium heat for 3 minutes, or until the egg moisture has evaporated. Add the broth and simmer gently for 9–10 minutes, or according to package directions, until the grains are tender but not disintegrating. Remove the pan from the heat and set the buckwheat aside.

4. Heat the remaining oil in the skillet. Add the onion and sauté over medium heat for 10 minutes. Season with salt and pepper, if using. Add the mushrooms and sauté for 5 minutes. Stir in the buckwheat, lemon juice, and most of the parsley.

5. Transfer the buckwheat mixture to four plates and arrange the squash on top. Sprinkle with the walnuts and the remaining parsley. Serve immediately.

PER SERVING: *662 cal / 42.1g fat / 7.8g sat fat / 67.6g carbs / 7.9g sugar / 10.3g fiber / 13.2g protein / 480mg sodium*

Zucchini Spaghetti

Zucchini create simple strips of spaghetti, which are then lightly cooked and tossed with pesto, roasted tomatoes, garlic, and feta cheese in this inspiring, nourishing dish. Toasted sunflower seeds add some vital vitamin E, too.

Serves 2
Prep: 30 minutes
Cook: 25–27 minutes

1 cup cherry tomatoes
4 garlic cloves, sliced
1 tablespoon olive oil
⅓ cup sunflower seeds
2 large zucchini
2 tablespoons fresh pesto
½ cup crumbled feta cheese
salt and pepper, optional
⅔ cup coarsely chopped fresh basil, to garnish

1. Preheat the oven to 400°F. Cut half of the cherry tomatoes in half horizontally and keep the rest whole. Put all the tomatoes and sliced garlic into a small roasting pan and drizzle with the olive oil. Shake well to coat and place in the preheated oven for 20 minutes.

2. Meanwhile, put a dry skillet over medium heat. Add the sunflower seeds and heat for 3–4 minutes, or until the seeds are just toasted. Set aside.

3. Now make your zucchini spaghetti. Lay a four-sided box grater on its side and grate the length of the zucchini into long strands. Try not to be firm—a loose grip makes this easier.

4. Bring a saucepan of water to a boil and add the zucchini strips. Cook for 1–2 minutes before draining thoroughly in a colander, gently squeezing any excess water away with the back of a spoon. Return the spaghetti to the pan and stir through the pesto. Season with salt and pepper, if using.

5. Stir two-thirds of the roasted tomato mixture, half of the sunflower seeds, and half of the crumbled feta into the spaghetti and divide the mixture between two plates. Top with the remaining tomatoes, sunflower seeds, and feta. Garnish with the basil and a sprinkling of black pepper, if using. Serve immediately.

PER SERVING: *464 cal / 37.8g fat / 9.7g sat fat / 19.9g carbs / 10.9g sugar / 6g fiber / 16.7g protein / 600mg sodium*

Raw Shoot & Seed-Packed Salad

Serves 6
Prep: 20 minutes
Cook: No cooking

4 cups mixed seed and bean sprouts
    (about 8 ounces), such as alfalfa,
    mung beans, soybeans, adzuki beans,
    chickpeas, and/or radish seeds
3 tablespoons pumpkin seeds
3 tablespoons sunflower seeds
3 tablespoons sesame seeds
1 crisp, sweet apple, such as Pink Lady,
    cored and coarsely chopped
½ cup coarsely chopped dried apricots
finely grated zest and juice of 1 lemon
½ cup coarsely chopped walnuts
2 tablespoons walnut oil

Help your body to rebalance with this nutritious and delicious meat-free, gluten-free salad. Bursting with healthy sprouted and dried seeds, walnuts, and fruit, this excellent salad is tossed together in a light, lemony dressing.

1. Put the seed and bean sprouts, pumpkin seeds, sunflower seeds, and sesame seeds into a large bowl. Stir in the apple, dried apricots, lemon zest, and walnuts.

2. To make the dressing, put the lemon juice and oil in a small bowl and mix together with a fork.

3. Stir the dressing into the salad, then serve immediately.

PER SERVING: *221 cal / 16.4g fat / 1.8g sat fat / 17.1g carbs / 11g sugar / 3.9g fiber / 5.8g protein / trace sodium*

Black Bean & Quinoa Burritos

Makes 8
Prep: 25–30 minutes, plus standing
Cook: 30–35 minutes

⅓ cup red quinoa, rinsed

⅔ cup water

2 tablespoons vegetable oil

1 red onion, diced

1 fresh green chile, seeded and diced

1 small red bell pepper,
    seeded and diced

1 (15-ounce) can black beans,
    drained and rinsed

juice of 1 lime

¼ cup chopped fresh cilantro

2 tomatoes

8 corn tortillas, warmed

1 cup shredded cheddar cheese

1½ cups shredded romaine lettuce

salt and pepper, optional

Quinoa and black beans boost the protein and fiber in these excellent burritos, finished with salsa and calcium-rich cheese.

1. Put the quinoa into a saucepan with the water. Bring to a boil, then cover and simmer over low heat for 15 minutes, or according to the package directions. Remove from the heat, but keep the pan covered for an additional 5 minutes to let the grains swell. Fluff up with a fork and set aside.

2. Heat the oil in a large skillet. Sauté half of the onion, half of the chile, and all of the red bell pepper until soft. Add the beans, cooked quinoa, and half of the lime juice and cilantro. Cook, stirring, for a few minutes, then season with salt and pepper, if using.

3. Halve the tomatoes and scoop out the seeds. Add the seeds to the bean mixture. Dice the tomato flesh and put into a bowl with the remaining cilantro, onion, chile, lime juice, and salt, if using. Stir.

4. Put ⅓ cup of the bean mixture on top of each tortilla. Sprinkle with the tomato salsa, the cheese, and lettuce. Fold the end and sides over the filling, roll up, and serve immediately.

PER BURRITO: *291 cal / 11.4g fat / 4.7g sat fat / 34.3g carbs / 4.5g sugar / 5.8g fiber / 11.4g protein / 280mg sodium*

Eggplants Stuffed with Bulgur Wheat

A good source of vitamins, minerals, and fiber, purple-skinned eggplants are great for stuffing and work well with spices in this wholesome dish. Fiber-rich bulgur wheat provides a good basis for the herb-filled vegetable stuffing, too.

Serves 4
Prep: 35 minutes, plus resting
Cook: 50 minutes

1 teaspoon ground cumin

1 teaspoon ground coriander

1 teaspoon paprika

1 teaspoon crushed red pepper flakes

2 tablespoons olive oil

2 eggplants, cut in half lengthwise

1 red onion, coarsely chopped

2 garlic cloves, chopped

1 cup bulgur wheat

1 cup vegetable broth

3 tablespoons coarsely chopped fresh cilantro

3 tablespoons coarsely chopped fresh mint

1 cup crumbled feta cheese

⅓ cup slivered almonds, toasted

1½ tablespoons lemon juice

2 teaspoons pomegranate molasses

salt and pepper, optional

1 tablespoon chopped fresh mint, to garnish

1 teaspoon pomegranate molasses, to garnish

½ cup Greek-style plain yogurt, to garnish

¼ cup pomegranate seeds, to garnish

1. Preheat the oven to 350°F. Mix the cumin, ground coriander, paprika, crushed red pepper flakes, and 1½ tablespoons of olive oil in a small bowl. Use a sharp knife to slice the eggplant flesh in a diagonal, crisscross pattern, being careful not to pierce the skin. Drizzle the cumin mixture over the eggplants and let it sink into the sliced pattern. Place the eggplant halves on a baking sheet and roast in the preheated oven for 35 minutes.

PER SERVING: *451 cal / 20.7g fat / 7.3g sat fat / 55.2g carbs / 12.6g sugar / 18.6g fiber / 17.5g protein / 560mg sodium*

2. Meanwhile, heat the remaining half a tablespoon of olive oil in a large skillet over medium heat. Add the onion and garlic and sauté for 3–4 minutes, or until softened. Reduce the heat, add the bulgur wheat, and stir well. Reduce the heat to low, pour the vegetable broth over the grains, and continue to stir until the liquid has been absorbed. Remove this mixture from the pan and transfer to a large bowl.

3. Remove the eggplants from the oven and let rest for 10 minutes, or until cool enough to handle. Keep the oven on. Using a tablespoon, scoop out the center of the eggplants, leaving a clear edge to support the filling.

4. Add the eggplant flesh to the bulgur mixture. Stir in the fresh cilantro, mint, feta, almonds, lemon juice, and pomegranate molasses. Stir well and season with salt and pepper, if using.

5. Divide the stuffing between the eggplants and return to the oven for 15 minutes. Serve immediately, garnished with the fresh mint, molasses, yogurt, and pomegranate seeds.

Butternut Squash
& Lentil Stew

Serves 4

Prep: 20 minutes
Cook: 35 minutes

1 tablespoon olive oil

1 onion, diced

3 garlic cloves, finely chopped

2 tablespoons tomato paste

2 teaspoons ground cumin

1 teaspoon ground cinnamon

1 teaspoon salt

¼ teaspoon cayenne pepper

½ butternut squash, peeled,
    seeded, and cut into bite-size pieces

½ cup brown lentils

2 cups vegetable broth

1 tablespoon lemon juice

¼ cup plain yogurt, to garnish

2 tablespoons finely chopped
    fresh cilantro, to garnish

2 tablespoons slivered almonds,
    to garnish

Naturally low in fat, lentils are packed with fiber and protein and are a good source of iron and other minerals. Teamed up with antioxidant-rich butternut squash, this tasty vegetarian stew packs a powerful nutrient punch.

1. Heat the oil in a large saucepan over medium–high heat. Add the onion and garlic and cook, stirring occasionally, for about 5 minutes, or until soft.

2. Add the tomato paste, cumin, cinnamon, salt, and cayenne and give it a quick stir. Add the squash, lentils, and broth to the pan and bring to a boil.

3. Reduce the heat to low and simmer, uncovered and stirring occasionally, for about 25 minutes, or until the squash and lentils are tender.

4. Just before serving, stir in the lemon juice. Serve hot, garnished with a dollop of the yogurt and a sprinkling of cilantro and slivered almonds.

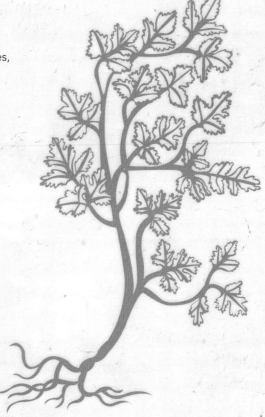

Multigrain & Seed Sprouts Salad

Serves 4
Prep: 30–35 minutes, plus cooling
Cook: 30–35 minutes

3 cups vegetable broth
¼ cup wild rice
¾ cup bulgur wheat
⅔ cup quinoa
2 zucchini, diagonally sliced
4 scallions, halved lengthwise
¼ cup olive oil
juice of ½ lemon
1 teaspoon cumin seeds, coarsely crushed
⅓ cup coarsely chopped fresh
    flat-leaf parsley
½ cup mixed seed sprouts,
    such as alfalfa and radish sprouts
salt and pepper, optional

Dressing
finely grated zest and juice
    of ½ unwaxed lemon
finely grated zest and juice of 1 lime
1 teaspoon honey

Health-giving grains, plenty of grilled vegetables, plus vitamin-rich seed sprouts are packed into this satisfying and sustaining salad. A light and zesty lemon and lime dressing brings it all together perfectly.

1. Bring the broth to a boil in a saucepan, add the rice, and simmer for 5 minutes. Add the bulgur wheat and simmer for an additional 5 minutes. Add the quinoa and simmer for 10–12 minutes, or prepare according to the package directions, until all the grains are tender. Drain off and discard the broth and spoon the grains into a salad bowl.

2. To make the dressing, put the lemon and lime zest and juices, honey, and 2 tablespoons of the olive oil into a screw-top jar. Season with salt and pepper, if using, screw on the lid, and shake well. Drizzle the dressing over the grains, toss gently together, then let cool.

3. Meanwhile, mix the zucchini and scallions with the remaining 2 tablespoons of olive oil, the lemon juice, and cumin and season with salt and pepper, if using.

4. Preheat a ridged grill pan over high heat. Add the zucchini and scallions to the hot pan and cook for 1–2 minutes on each side, or until browned. Transfer to a plate and let cool. Serve the grains on four plates and top with the grilled vegetables. Top with the parsley and seed sprouts and serve.

Cashew & Chickpea Curry

Serves 4
Prep: 15 minutes
Cook: 40–45 minutes

1 medium-large Yukon gold or red-skinned
   potato, chopped into bite-size pieces
3 tablespoons vegetable oil
1 onion, chopped
2 garlic cloves, chopped
1¼-inch piece fresh ginger,
   finely chopped
1 teaspoon cumin seeds
1 teaspoon chili powder
½ teaspoon ground turmeric
½ teaspoon ground cinnamon
1 (15-ounce) can chickpeas,
   drained and rinsed
1¼ cups cashew nuts
1½ cups vegetable broth
⅓ cup coconut milk
1 tablespoon chopped fresh cilantro,
   to garnish
2 cups freshly cooked rice, to serve

Crammed with chickpeas and cashew nuts, this tasty curry is brimming with essential nutrients, including fiber and protein.

1. Put the potato chunks into a large saucepan of boiling water and cook for 10–15 minutes, until tender but still firm.

2. Heat the oil in a large saucepan over medium heat. Sauté the onion, garlic, ginger, cumin seeds, chili powder, turmeric, and cinnamon for 5 minutes, or until the onion is soft and translucent.

3. Stir in the boiled potato with the chickpeas and cashews, and cook for an additional 3 minutes. Stir in the broth and coconut milk. Reduce the heat to low and continue to cook for 15 minutes, or until thick and creamy.

4. Garnish with cilantro and serve immediately with the freshly cooked rice on the side.

PER SERVING: *720 cal / 44.7g fat / 19.5g sat fat / 62.8g carbs / 8.8g sugar / 7.3g fiber / 16.5g protein / 360mg sodium*

Whole Baked Cauliflower

Low-fat, cholesterol-free, and loaded with vitamin C, cauliflower is baked whole and served with a tasty tomato, olive, and caper sauce. Fiber and protein-packed lima beans add to the mix in this warming dish.

Serves 4
Prep: 20–25 minutes
Cook: 1 hour

1 tablespoon olive oil
2 onions, finely sliced
4 garlic cloves, chopped
2 tablespoons red wine vinegar
pinch of light brown sugar
¾ cup pitted black ripe olives
2 tablespoons capers
3 tablespoons coarsely chopped fresh basil
1 (28-ounce) can diced tomatoes
1 (15-ounce) can lima beans, drained and rinsed
⅔ cup vegetable broth
1 large head of cauliflower, leaves trimmed
salt and pepper, optional
2 tablespoons basil sprigs, to garnish

1. Heat the olive oil in a saucepan that is large enough to contain the whole cauliflower.

2. Add the onions and garlic and sauté over medium heat, until soft and translucent. Stir in the vinegar, brown sugar, black olives, capers, and basil and heat through for an additional 2–3 minutes. Pour in the tomatoes, lima beans, and vegetable broth. Stir well and bring the saucepan to a simmer for 5–6 minutes, stirring occasionally.

3. Sit the cauliflower head upside down on a cutting board and, using a sharp knife, carefully cut the tough stem away. Place the cauliflower into the center of the tomato sauce, pushing it down so half is covered by the sauce. Season with salt and pepper, if using.

4. Reduce the heat to low, cover, and simmer for about 45 minutes, or until the cauliflower is tender. Carefully stir once or twice during cooking to prevent the sauce from catching on the bottom of the pan. Serve immediately, garnished with basil.

PER SERVING: *242 cal / 7.3g fat / 1g sat fat / 34.6g carbs / 14.2g sugar / 9.6g fiber / 11.5g protein / 440mg sodium*

Brown Rice Risotto Primavera

Serves 4

Prep: 25 minutes
Cook: 45 minutes

5 cups vegetable broth

1 tablespoon olive oil

1 large leek, thinly sliced, white
and green slices kept separate

2 garlic cloves, finely chopped

1⅓ cups short-grain brown rice

16 baby carrots (about 5½ ounces),
tops trimmed, halved lengthwise

8 thin asparagus spears, trimmed

1 zucchini, cut into cubes

2 tablespoons butter

¾ cup finely grated Parmesan cheese

2¼ cups mixed baby spinach,
watercress, and arugula leaves

Loaded with fresh spring vegetables for vitality, this brown rice risotto provides a delicious and balanced meat-free meal.

1. Bring the broth to a boil in a saucepan.

2. Meanwhile, heat the oil in a large skillet over medium heat. Add the white leek slices and garlic and cook for 3–4 minutes, or until softened but not browned.

3. Stir the rice into the pan and cook for 1 minute. Pour in half of the hot broth, bring back to a boil, then cover and simmer for 15 minutes.

4. Add the carrots and half of the remaining broth and stir again. Cover and cook for 15 minutes.

5. Add the green leek slices, asparagus, and zucchini to the rice, then add a little extra broth. Replace the lid and cook for 5–6 minutes, or until the vegetables and rice are just tender.

6. Remove from the heat, stir in the butter and two-thirds of the cheese, and add a little more broth, if needed. Top with the mixed greens, cover with the lid, and warm through for 1–2 minutes, or until the greens are just beginning to wilt.

7. Spoon the risotto into shallow bowls, sprinkle with the remaining cheese, and serve immediately.

PER SERVING: *433 cal / 16.8g fat / 8.1g sat fat / 59.6g carbs / 5.4g sugar / 5g fiber / 13.6g protein / 1480mg sodium*

Tagliatelle with Roasted Pumpkin

Homemade pesto is hard to beat, especially this walnut-loaded version, rich in essential omega-3 fatty acids and heart-healthy monounsaturated fat. It's also delicious tossed with whole-wheat tagliatelle and roasted pumpkin.

Serves 4

Prep: 35–40 minutes
Cook: 30–35 minutes

½ small pumpkin or 1 large butternut squash (about 2¼ pounds), seeded, peeled, and cut into ¾-inch slices
2 tablespoons virgin olive oil
1 pound fresh whole-wheat tagliatelle
salt and pepper, optional
1 tablespoon thinly shaved Parmesan cheese, to serve

Walnut pesto

¾ cup walnut pieces
⅓ cup virgin olive oil
¼ cup fresh basil
¼ cup Parmesan cheese shavings
2½ cups arugula

1. Preheat the oven to 400°F. Arrange the pumpkin on a large baking sheet in a single layer. Drizzle with the oil and season with salt and pepper, if using. Roast for 20–25 minutes, or until just tender.

2. Meanwhile, to make the pesto, put the walnuts into a large skillet and toast for 2–3 minutes, or until just beginning to brown. Transfer to a food processor or blender, pour in the oil, and process until coarsely ground. Add the basil, cheese, and half of the arugula and process again until you have a coarse pesto.

3. Bring a large saucepan of water to a boil, add the tagliatelle, and cook for 3–4 minutes, or according to the package directions, until al dente.

4. Drain the pasta and pour a little of the cooking water into a small bowl. Return the pasta to the pan. Cut the pumpkin into cubes and add this to the pasta. Drizzle with the pesto and gently toss together, adding a little of the reserved pasta water, if needed, to loosen the sauce. Top with the remaining arugula.

5. Spoon into bowls and serve immediately, with the Parmesan cheese on top.

High-Fiber Green Lentil & Egg Salad

Serves 4
Prep: 30 minutes, plus cooling
Cook: 40–45 minutes

3½ cups vegetable broth

2 bay leaves

1 cinnamon stick, halved

2 leeks plus the bottom half of 1 leek

1 cup dried green lentils,
  rinsed and drained

3 tablespoons olive oil

2 garlic cloves, finely chopped

4 eggs

2 tablespoons capers,
  drained and chopped

3 cups baby spinach

¼ cup fresh flat-leaf parsley,
  coarsely chopped

Dressing

2 tablespoons red wine vinegar

1 teaspoon Dijon mustard

salt and pepper, optional

Packed with fiber, lentils add a healthy, low-fat source of protein to this tempting mixed vegetable and egg salad, finished with a drizzle of piquant mustard dressing and sprinkled with antioxidant-rich fresh parsley.

1. Put the broth, bay, and cinnamon into a saucepan and bring just to a boil. Put the bottom half of leek and the lentils into the pan. Cover and simmer for 25 minutes, or according to the package directions, until the lentils are tender and nearly all the broth has been absorbed. Top up with a little boiling water during cooking, if needed. Drain the lentils, transfer to a salad bowl, and discard the cooked leek, bay leaves, and cinnamon stick.

2. Meanwhile, thinly slice the whole leeks. Heat 1 tablespoon of olive oil in a skillet over medium heat. Add the sliced leeks and the garlic, and sauté for 3–4 minutes, stirring, until just beginning to soften. Remove from the heat and let cool.

3. Put the eggs in a saucepan and pour in enough cold water to cover them by ½ inch. Bring to a boil, then reduce the heat and boil for 8 minutes. Drain immediately, cool by quickly placing the eggs under cold running water, then peel and cut into quarters.

4. To make the dressing, put the vinegar, remaining 2 tablespoons of oil, and the mustard into a screw-top jar. Season with salt and pepper, if using, screw on the lid, and shake well.

5. Drizzle the dressing over the lentils and toss gently together. Top with the sliced leek mixture, capers, and spinach. Arrange the hard-boiled eggs over the salad, sprinkle with the chopped parsley, and serve immediately.

Kale & Lima Bean Casserole

Served bubbling hot, this filling casserole of nourishing, nutrient-packed lima beans, onions, tomatoes, and kale, finished with a flurry of diced avocado, creates a really wholesome meal, perfect for a chilly winter's day.

Serves 6

Prep: 25 minutes, plus overnight soaking
Cook: 1¾–2 hours

1½ cups dried lima beans, soaked overnight

1 tablespoon cumin seeds

2 teaspoons dried oregano

3 tablespoons peanut oil

2 onions, chopped

2 garlic cloves, thinly sliced

1–3 fresh red or green chiles, seeded and sliced

1 (14½-ounce) can diced tomatoes

2 cups vegetable broth

2⅔ cups shredded kale

⅓ cup chopped fresh cilantro

juice of 1 lime

salt and pepper, optional

2 avocados, cubed and tossed with
   1 teaspoon lime juice, to garnish

½ red onion, sliced, to garnish

1. Drain the beans, put them into a large saucepan, and cover with water. Bring to a boil, boil for 15 minutes, then simmer for 30–45 minutes, until tender but not disintegrating. Drain and set aside.

2. Put the cumin seeds into a small, dry skillet over medium heat and heat until fragrant. Add the oregano, cook for a few seconds, then immediately remove the mixture from the pan.

3. Lightly crush the mixture in a mortar with a pestle.

4. Heat the oil in a large, flameproof casserole dish over medium heat. Add the chopped onions and the spice-and-herb mixture. Sauté for 5 minutes, until the onions are translucent. Add the garlic and chiles and sauté for an additional 2 minutes.

5. Stir the tomatoes, beans, and broth into the casserole. Season with salt and pepper, if using, and bring to a boil. Reduce the heat, cover, and simmer for 30 minutes, stirring occasionally.

6. Increase the heat and stir in the kale. Simmer, uncovered, for 7 minutes, or until tender but still brightly colored. Stir in the cilantro and lime juice.

7. Ladle into soup bowls, garnish with the avocado and red onion, and serve immediately.

PER SERVING: *400 cal / 15.8g fat / 2.7g sat fat / 52.5g carbs / 6.9g sugar / 14.4g fiber / 17.8g protein / 320mg sodium*

Beet Burgers in Buns

Makes 5
Prep: 30 minutes,
  plus standing and chilling
Cook: 35–40 minutes

½ cup millet, rinsed and drained
¾ cup water
2 raw beets, grated
½ carrot, grated
1 zucchini, grated
½ cup finely chopped walnuts
2 tablespoons apple cider vinegar
2 tablespoons olive oil
1 egg, beaten
2 tablespoons cornstarch
2 tablespoons olive oil, for frying
salt and pepper, optional
5 multigrain hamburger buns,
  halved, to serve
5 lettuce leaves, to serve

Yogurt sauce
1 cup plain yogurt
2 garlic cloves, finely chopped

Wow your taste buds with these tasty grilled millet and mixed vegetable burgers. Stuffed into multigrain hamburger buns and served with a low-fat garlic yogurt sauce, they make an excellent lunch or dinner for sharing.

1. Put the millet, water, and salt, if using, in a small saucepan. Bring to a simmer over medium heat, then reduce the heat to low, cover, and cook for 20–25 minutes, or according to the package directions, until tender. Remove from the heat and let stand for 5 minutes, covered with a lid.

2. Put the beets, carrot, zucchini, and walnuts into a large bowl. Add the millet, vinegar, oil, and salt and pepper, if using, and mix well to combine. Add the egg and cornstarch, mix again, then cover and chill in the refrigerator for 2 hours.

3. Meanwhile, to make the yogurt sauce, put the yogurt in a fine strainer over a bowl and let drain for at least 30 minutes. Stir in the garlic and season with salt and pepper, if using.

4. Spoon the beet mixture into five mounds on a cutting board, then squeeze them into patties using wet hands. Place a ridged grill pan or large skillet over medium heat and coat with olive oil. Add the patties and cook for 10 minutes, or until browned, turning halfway through.

5. Top the bottom of each bun with a spoonful of the yogurt sauce. Place the burgers on top, then the lettuce, then the bun lid. Serve immediately.

PER BURGER IN BUN: *498 cal / 24.6g fat / 4.2g sat fat / 55g carbs / 9.6g sugar / 8.5g fiber / 16g protein / 320mg sodium*

181

Winter Squash, Feta & Adzuki Bean Packages

Served crisp, golden, and freshly baked from the oven, these fantastic feta, bean, and winter squash-packed phyllo packages provide a wholesome, meat-free lunch or dinner for all the family to enjoy.

Serves 6
Prep: 40 minutes
Cook: 45–50 minutes

4 cups ¾-inch winter squash cubes (about 1 pound), such as buttercup squash, butternut squash, acorn squash, or pumpkin

4 shallots, quartered

1 teaspoon smoked paprika

1 tablespoon olive oil

¾ cup drained and rinsed, canned adzuki beans

2 tablespoons coarsely chopped parsley

zest of 1 lemon

⅔ cup crumbled feta cheese

3 sheets of phyllo pastry, thawed if frozen

3½ tablespoons butter, melted

pepper, optional

1 tablespoon snipped watercress, to garnish

green salad, to serve, optional

1. Preheat the oven to 400°F. Put the winter squash and shallots into a shallow roasting pan in an even layer and sprinkle with the paprika. Drizzle with the olive oil and mix well. Roast in the preheated oven for 20–25 minutes, or until the squash is slightly golden and soft. Keep the oven on.

2. Put the squash mixture into a large bowl. Using a potato masher, mash until the cubes have broken down. Stir in the adzuki beans, parsley, lemon zest, and feta cheese. Mix until all the ingredients are well combined. Season with pepper, if using.

3. Cut a phyllo sheet in half to create two long lengths and brush one pastry length all over with melted butter. Cover the remaining pastry with a damp dish towel to keep it fresh.

4. Spoon one-sixth of the squash mixture on one end of the pastry length. Fold this end up to meet one side, starting the shape of a triangle. Fold the bottom point of the pastry up, sealing in the filling, then complete the triangle by folding again in the opposite direction. Keep folding until you reach the top and lightly brush with a little more melted butter. Repeat with the other sheets of phyllo until you have six triangles.

5. Place the packages on a baking sheet and cook for 25 minutes, or until golden. Garnish with watercress and serve immediately with a green salad, if desired.

PER SERVING: 213 cal / 13.4g fat / 7.3g sat fat / 18.4g carbs / 2.6g sugar / 1.9g fiber / 6g protein / 280mg sodium

Miso & Tofu Salad

This tempting salad of broiled sesame-sprinkled tofu, paired with nourishing green vegetables for vitality, boasts a fusion of fresh flavors from afar and creates an appealing meat-free meal for friends.

Serves 4

Prep: 25 minutes
Cook: 8–10 minutes

14 ounces firm tofu, drained and cut into ½-inch slices

1 tablespoon sesame seeds

1 cup thinly sliced snow peas

1 cup bean sprouts

10 asparagus spears, trimmed and cut into long, thin slices

1 zucchini, cut into matchsticks

1 small butterhead lettuce, leaves separated and cut into long slices

⅓ cup coarsely chopped fresh cilantro

1⅓ cups mixed seed sprouts, such as alfalfa and radish sprouts

Dressing

3 tablespoons rice wine vinegar

2 tablespoons soy sauce

3 tablespoons sunflower oil

1 tablespoon sweet white miso

2 garlic cloves, finely chopped

1. To make the dressing, put the vinegar and soy sauce into a screw-top jar, then add the oil, miso, and garlic. Screw on the lid and shake well.

2. Preheat the broiler to high and line the broiler pan with aluminum foil. Put the tofu on the foil in a single layer. Mark crisscross lines over each slice, using a knife, then sprinkle with the sesame seeds. Spoon half of the dressing over the tofu, then broil for 8–10 minutes, turning once, until browned.

3. Put the snow peas, bean sprouts, asparagus, zucchini, and lettuce on a serving plate. Pour the remaining dressing over the vegetables and toss gently together. Sprinkle with the cilantro and sprouts, then top with the hot tofu, drizzle with any pan juices, and serve immediately.

PER SERVING: 236 cal / 15g fat / 1.7g sat fat / 15.4g carbs / 8.4g sugar / 4.8g fiber / 13.2g protein / 640mg sodium

Stuffed Red Bell Peppers

Savor the fine flavor of these vibrant red vitamin-packed bell peppers, stuffed with an energy-giving medley of lean ground beef, assorted beans, vegetables, and spices. Perfect for a sustaining weekend meal.

Serves 4

Prep: 25 minutes
Cook: 1 hour

4 large red bell peppers, stems left on, halved
    lengthwise and seeded
1 tablespoon olive oil
1 red onion, finely chopped
14 ounces ground round or ground sirloin beef
2 garlic cloves, finely chopped
¼ teaspoon smoked hot paprika or chili powder
1 teaspoon ground cumin
1 (15-ounce) can chickpeas, drained and rinsed
2 cups cooked green lentils
1 (14¼-ounce) can diced tomatoes
½ cup beef broth
salt and pepper, optional
¾ cup low-fat Greek-style plain yogurt, optional
⅓ cup coarsely chopped fresh mint
¼ cup coarsely chopped fresh flat-leaf parsley

1. Preheat the oven to 350°F. Arrange the bell peppers, cut side up, in a roasting pan.

2. Heat the oil in a skillet over medium heat. Add the red onion, ground beef, and garlic and cook, stirring and breaking up the meat, for 5 minutes, or until evenly browned.

3. Stir in the paprika and cumin, then the chickpeas, lentils, tomatoes, and broth. Season with salt and pepper, if using, then increase the heat to high and bring to a boil. Remove from the heat.

4. Spoon the meat mixture into the bell peppers, cover the dish with aluminum foil, then bake for 50 minutes, or until the peppers are tender and the meat is cooked.

5. Remove the foil, top each pepper with a spoonful of yogurt, if using, then sprinkle generously with the mint and parsley and serve immediately.

PER SERVING: 385 cal / 10.8g fat / 3g sat fat / 35g carbs / 14.3g sugar / 10.7g fiber / 32.5g protein / 200mg sodium

Spanish Vegetable Stew

Serves 4
Prep: 25 minutes
Cook: 55 minutes

2 tablespoons virgin olive oil

1 onion, coarsely chopped

1 eggplant, coarsely chopped

½ teaspoon smoked hot paprika

2 garlic cloves, finely chopped

1 large red bell pepper, seeded
  and coarsely chopped

9 ounces baby new potatoes,
  unpeeled and any larger ones halved

7 plum tomatoes (about 1 pound),
  peeled and coarsely chopped

1 (15-ounce) navy beans,
  drained and rinsed

⅔ cup vegetable broth

2 sprigs of fresh rosemary

2 zucchini, coarsely chopped

salt and pepper, optional

This wholesome and hearty Spanish stew is crammed with nutrient-dense vegetables and beans and fully flavored with warming smoked paprika and robust rosemary. Serve on its own or with fresh bread for a satisfying meal.

1. Preheat the oven to 400°F. Heat 1 tablespoon of the oil in a saucepan over medium heat. Add the onion and sauté for 5 minutes, or until softened. Add another tablespoon of oil, then add the eggplant and sauté, stirring, for 5 minutes, or until just beginning to soften and brown.

2. Stir in the smoked paprika and garlic, then the red bell pepper, potatoes, and tomatoes. Add the navy beans, broth, and rosemary, then season with salt and pepper, if using. Bring to a boil, cover, turn the heat down to medium–low, and simmer for 30 minutes, stirring from time to time.

3. Stir the zucchini into the stew, then cook, uncovered, for about 10 minutes, or until all the vegetables are tender and the sauce has reduced slightly.

4. Ladle the stew into shallow bowls, discard the rosemary sprigs, and serve immediately.

PER SERVING: *278 cal / 8.5g fat / 1.3g sat fat / 41.8g carbs / 13g sugar / 14.9g fiber / 10.4g protein / 160mg sodium*

Roasted Beet & Squash Salad

Raid your vegetable stash to make this scrumptious salad. Low-fat and loaded with vitamins, minerals, and antioxidants, beets and butternut squash add vitality and plenty of feel-good factor to this sustaining mixed grain salad.

Serves 4

Prep: 25 minutes
Cook: 30 minutes

5 raw beets (about 1 pound), green stems trimmed, peeled, and cut into ¾-inch cubes

3 cups ¾-inch butternut squash cubes

¼ cup olive oil

½ cup brown basmati or other long-grain rice

½ cup red Camargue or long-grain brown rice

½ cup quick-cooking farro

4 cups beet greens or other salad greens

salt and pepper, optional

Dressing

1 tablespoon flaxseed oil

2 tablespoons red wine vinegar

½ teaspoon smoked hot paprika

1 teaspoon fennel seeds, coarsely crushed

2 teaspoons tomato paste

1. Preheat the oven to 400°F. Put the beets and squash into a roasting pan, drizzle with half of the olive oil, and season with salt and pepper, if using. Roast for 30 minutes, or until just tender.

2. Meanwhile, put the basmati rice and red Camargue rice into a saucepan of boiling water. Bring back to a boil, then simmer, uncovered, for 15 minutes. Add the farro and cook for an additional 10 minutes, or until all the grains are tender. Drain and rinse, then transfer to a serving plate.

3. To make the dressing, put all the ingredients and the remaining 2 tablespoons of olive oil into a screw-top jar. Season with salt and pepper, if using, screw on the lid, and shake well. Drizzle the dressing over the rice mixture, then toss gently together.

4. Spoon the roasted vegetables over the grains and let cool. Toss gently together, then sprinkle with the beet greens and serve immediately.

PER SERVING: *528 cal / 19.2g fat / 2.5g sat fat / 64.9g carbs / 10.9g sugar / 10.1g fiber / 10.7g protein / 160mg sodium*

Mushroom Farro Risotto

Hearty whole-grain farro adds a delicious nutty flavor to this flavorful mushroom risotto. Flavored with garlic, shallots, and aromatic thyme, plus a handful of superfood spinach leaves, it provides a filling and nutritious meat-free meal.

Serves 4
Prep: 25 minutes
Cook: 50–55 minutes

1 cup farro
2 tablespoons olive oil
4 cups cremini mushrooms
5 shallots, finely chopped
4 garlic cloves, sliced
2 tablespoons fresh thyme leaves
3 cups vegetable broth
2½ cups baby spinach
¼ cup grated Parmesan cheese
pepper, optional
2 tablespoons coarsely chopped fresh flat-leaf parsley, to garnish
¼ cup plain yogurt, to serve

1. Bring a large saucepan of water to a boil. Add the farro to the pan and simmer gently for 15 minutes, to begin the cooking process. Drain the farro and set aside.

2. Meanwhile, add half of the olive oil to a large, deep skillet. Add the mushrooms and sauté over high heat for 2–3 minutes, or until they have softened. Remove the mushrooms from the pan and set aside on a plate.

3. Add the remaining olive oil to the skillet and, once hot, add the shallots, garlic, and thyme. Reduce the heat to medium and continue to sauté for a few minutes, until the shallots have softened but not browned.

PER SERVING: 303 cal / 11.1g fat / 3g sat fat / 43.6g carbs / 3.6g sugar / 4.3g fiber / 10.7g protein / 840mg sodium

4. Stir the softened farro through the shallot mixture and pour the broth over the mixture, in thirds, stirring well after each addition. Let simmer on low heat, stirring occasionally, for 30–35 minutes, or until the farro is soft but still has a little bite in the center and the liquid has all but disappeared. If the pan runs dry, add a little more water.

5. Once the farro is cooked, return the mushrooms to the pan with the spinach. Let the spinach wilt before stirring through the Parmesan. Season with pepper, if using. Serve in bowls, garnished with flat-leaf parsley and a dollop of plain yogurt.

Power-Packed
Protein

Spicy Steak with Roasted Squash

Lean and juicy high-protein tenderloin steaks are lightly grilled, then served with roasted vegetables and a pleasing piquant sauce to produce this tantalizing meal, excellent for a weekend dinner with family or friends.

Serves 4
Prep: 25–30 minutes
Cook: 35–40 minutes, plus resting

Roasted vegetables
1 butternut squash, cut into chunks
4 garlic cloves, finely chopped
4 large portobello mushrooms, cut into thick slices
½ cup finely chopped fresh sage leaves
2 tablespoons olive oil

Chimichurri sauce
½ cup fresh flat-leaf parsley
½ teaspoon dried oregano
2 garlic cloves
1 shallot, chopped
¼ teaspoon crushed red pepper flakes
grated zest and juice of ½ lemon
2 tablespoons red wine vinegar
2 tablespoons olive oil
2 tablespoons cold water

Steaks
4 tenderloin steaks, about 6 ounces each
1 tablespoon olive oil, for brushing
1 tablespoon olive oil, for drizzling
salt and pepper, optional

1. Preheat the oven to 400°F. Put the squash, garlic, mushrooms, and sage into a large roasting pan. Drizzle with the olive oil and mix well. Season with salt and pepper, if using, and roast in the preheated oven for 25–30 minutes, turning once halfway through the cooking time.

2. Meanwhile, make the sauce. Put all of the ingredients, except the water, into a bowl and blend, using a handheld blender or food processor. Carefully pour in the water, adding just enough to reach a spooning consistency. Set aside.

PER SERVING: 527 cal / 28.2g fat / 5.8g sat fat / 29.6g carbs / 6.2g sugar / 5g fiber / 44.2g protein / 120mg sodium

3. Brush the steaks with the olive oil and season with salt and pepper, if using. Place a heavy skillet or ridged grill pan over high heat and once smoking, add the steaks and reduce the heat to medium–high. Cook for 2–3 minutes on each side for medium–rare, or cook to your taste. Remove the steaks from the pan and let them rest for a few minutes before serving.

4. Cut the steaks into thick slices and serve on top of the roasted vegetables. Drizzle with the chimichurri sauce and the olive oil.

Chicken & Giant Couscous Salad

Serves 4
Prep: 35 minutes
Cook: 35–40 minutes

1½ cups giant whole-wheat couscous
4 cooked beets, diced
1 small red onion, finely chopped
8 cherry tomatoes, halved
1 pomegranate, halved and
    seeds removed and reserved
juice of 2 lemons
2 tablespoons flaxseed oil
2 tablespoons olive oil
4 teaspoons tomato paste
2 tablespoons coarsely chopped
    fresh mint
1 teaspoon black peppercorns,
    coarsely crushed
1 pound 2 ounces boneless, skinless
    chicken breasts, sliced
salt and pepper, optional

Low in fat and cholesterol-free, whole-wheat couscous provides a good source of fiber, so when it's combined with protein-packed chicken, plus nutrient-rich beets and pomegranate seeds, this salad bursts with natural goodness.

1. Put the couscous into a saucepan of boiling water. Bring back to a boil, then simmer for 6—8 minutes, or according to the package directions, until just tender. Drain into a strainer, rinse with cold water, then transfer to a salad bowl. Add the beets, then the onion, tomatoes, and pomegranate seeds.

2. To make the dressing, put the juice of 1 lemon, the flaxseed oil, half of the olive oil, and half of the tomato paste into a screw-top jar. Season with salt and pepper, if using, screw on the lid, and shake well. Drizzle the dressing over the salad, then sprinkle with the chopped mint and toss together.

3. Put the remaining lemon juice, olive oil, and tomato paste and the crushed peppercorns into a clean plastic bag, twist, and shake well. Add the chicken, seal, then shake until the chicken is evenly coated.

4. Preheat a ridged grill pan over high heat. Cook the chicken (in batches if necessary) in the hot pan for 10 minutes, turning once or twice, until cooked all the way through. Cut through the middle of a slice to check that the meat is no longer pink and any juices run clear. Arrange over the salad and serve.

PER SERVING: 503 cal / 18.9g fat / 2.3g sat fat / 51.4g carbs / 10.2g sugar / 7.7g fiber / 36.2g protein / 160mg sodium

Roasted Pork with Gingered Apples

Serves 4
Prep: 25 minutes, plus marinating
Cook: 55 minutes, plus resting

2 garlic cloves, crushed

¼ cup red wine

2 tablespoons light brown sugar

1 tablespoon soy sauce

1 teaspoon sesame oil

½ teaspoon ground cinnamon

¼ teaspoon ground cloves

1 star anise, broken into pieces

½ teaspoon pepper

12 ounces pork tenderloin

3¼ cups cooked green beans,
to serve

Gingered apples

4 cooking apples, such as
Granny Smiths, coarsely chopped

1 tablespoon rice vinegar

1 tablespoon packed light brown sugar

¼ cup apple juice

1 tablespoon finely chopped fresh ginger

Roasted, marinated lean pork tenderloin, accompanied by a homemade applesauce with a ginger twist, creates this appealing meal. Along with its warm, spicy flavor, fresh ginger is also a helpful digestive aid.

1. In a large bowl, combine the garlic, wine, brown sugar, soy sauce, sesame oil, cinnamon, cloves, star anise, and pepper. Add the pork and toss to coat. Cover and refrigerate overnight.

2. Preheat the oven to 375°F. Heat a nonstick skillet over high heat. Remove the pork from the marinade and sear in the hot pan. Cook for about 8 minutes, or until browned on all sides. Transfer the pork to an ovenproof dish and drizzle with half of the marinade. Roast in the preheated oven for 15 minutes.

3. Turn the meat, drizzle the remaining marinade over the top, and roast for 30 minutes, or until cooked through (insert the tip of a sharp knife into the center of the meat and check that there is no pink meat).

4. Meanwhile, make the gingered apples. In a saucepan, combine all the ingredients and cook over medium–high heat, until the liquid begins to boil. Reduce the heat to medium–low and simmer, stirring occasionally, for about 20 minutes, or until the apples are soft.

5. Remove the pork from the oven and set aside to rest for 5 minutes. Slice the meat and serve with the apples and green beans.

PER SERVING: 324 cal / 3.6g fat / 0.8g sat fat / 53.4g carbs / 37.4g sugar / 9g fiber / 20.7g protein / 440mg sodium

Tuna with Bok Choy & Soba Noodles

Tasty, fresh tuna steaks team up with vitamin-rich bok choy and buckwheat soba noodles to make this revitalizing Japanese-style dish for two that is full of fresh, natural flavors and appeal.

Serves 2

Prep: 20–25 minutes
Cook: 20 minutes

½ head of bok choy
4 ounces soba noodles
2 tuna steaks, about 6 ounces each and ½ inch thick
1 tablespoon peanut oil, for brushing
2 tablespoons peanut oil
2 slices fresh ginger, cut into matchsticks
½–1 fresh red chile, seeded and thinly sliced
4 scallions, some green included, thickly sliced diagonally
1 cup frozen edamame (soybeans), thawed
2 tablespoons chicken broth
squeeze of lime juice
3 tablespoons chopped fresh cilantro
salt and pepper, optional

1. Slice the bok choy stems into bite-size pieces. Slice the leaves into broad ribbons.

2. Bring a large saucepan of water to a boil. Add the noodles, bring back to a boil, and cook for 5–6 minutes, or according to the package directions, until just tender. Drain, reserving the cooking water. Rinse the noodles well and set aside. Return the reserved water to the pan and keep warm over low heat.

3. Meanwhile, cut the tuna steaks into thirds. Brush with oil and season with salt and pepper, if using. Heat a ridged grill pan over high heat. Add the tuna and cook for 2–2½ minutes on each side. Transfer to a plate and set aside in a warm place.

4. Heat a wok over medium–high heat. Add the oil and sizzle the ginger, chile, and scallions for a few seconds.

5. Add the bok choy stems, edamame (soybeans), and broth and stir-fry for 3 minutes. Add the bok choy leaves and stir-fry for an additional minute. Add the lime juice and cilantro, then season to taste with salt and pepper, if using.

6. Reheat the noodles in the cooking water, then drain thoroughly. Divide the noodles between two plates, add the vegetables, and arrange the tuna on top. Serve immediately.

PER SERVING: *717 cal / 27.2g fat / 4.2g sat fat / 53.2g carbs / 7.1g sugar / 7.4g fiber / 63.8g protein / 720mg sodium*

Squid with Saffron Mayonnaise

Serves 2

Prep: 30–35 minutes,
  plus soaking and chilling
Cook: 14–16 minutes

1 pound 2 ounces whole small squid,
  skinned, cleaned, and gutted
3 tablespoons cornstarch
vegetable oil, for deep-frying
salt and pepper, optional
2 lemon wedges, to serve, optional

Saffron mayonnaise

small pinch of saffron strands
1 teaspoon lukewarm water
3 tablespoons whole egg mayonnaise
½ small garlic clove, finely chopped

Salad

head of red endive, leaves separated
10 sprigs of watercress
1 tablespoon Parmesan cheese shavings
juice of ¼ lemon
1 tablespoon extra virgin olive oil

Fresh squid provides a rich source of protein and a good dose of vitamins and minerals. Deep-fried, then served with saffron mayonnaise and a simple salad, this decadent dish creates a mouthwatering meal for two.

1. To make the flavored mayonnaise, put the saffron and water in a small bowl and let soak for 5 minutes. Stir during the soaking to release the flavor. Meanwhile, put the mayonnaise and garlic into a bowl and mix well. When the saffron has turned the water vibrant yellow, discard the saffron strands and stir the liquid into the mayonnaise. Transfer to two dipping bowls, cover with plastic wrap, and chill in the refrigerator.

2. To make the salad, put the endive and watercress into a large bowl, then sprinkle with the cheese. Put the lemon juice and oil into a small bowl and mix well with a fork.

3. Slice the squid body into ½-inch circles and cut the tentacles in half. Wash under cold running water, then dry on paper towels. Put the cornstarch onto a plate, season with salt and pepper, if using, and toss the squid lightly in the mixture until thoroughly coated.

4. Heat the oil in a deep, heavy saucepan, being careful not to fill the pan too high. To test whether it is hot enough, drop in a small cube of bread. If it takes about 30 seconds to turn golden, the oil is ready.

5. Cook the squid in two batches, because too much squid in the pan will make the oil temperature drop. Carefully add half the squid to the oil and cook for 2–3 minutes, until the coating is just tinged golden.

6. Using a slotted spoon, transfer the cooked squid to paper towels to drain, then keep warm in the oven while you cook the second batch.

7. Season the squid with salt and pepper, if using. Pour the dressing over the salad. Serve the squid immediately with the salad and saffron mayonnaise, and lemon wedges for squeezing over the squid, if using.

PER SERVING: *626 cal / 38.4g fat / 7g sat fat / 34.9g carbs / 1.6g sugar / 1.8g fiber / 33.8g protein / 320mg sodium*

Spiced Turkey Stew with Couscous

Just right for a chilly winter day, recharge your batteries with this warming, wholesome stew of lean turkey and vibrant red, antioxidant-rich vegetables, served with whole-grain couscous and sprinkled with fresh herbs.

Serves 4
Prep: 25 minutes
Cook: 25 minutes

1 tablespoon virgin olive oil
1 pound 2 ounces skinless and boneless turkey breasts,
    cut into ¾-inch pieces
1 onion, coarsely chopped
2 garlic cloves, finely chopped
1 red and 1 orange bell pepper, seeded and coarsely chopped
4 tomatoes (about 1 pound), coarsely chopped
1 teaspoon cumin seeds, coarsely crushed
1 teaspoon paprika
finely grated zest and juice of 1 lemon
salt and pepper, optional

To serve
1 cup whole-grain giant couscous
2 tablespoons coarsely chopped fresh flat-leaf parsley
2 tablespoons coarsely chopped fresh cilantro

1. Heat the oil in a large skillet over medium heat. Add the turkey, a few pieces at a time, then add the onion. Cook, stirring, for 5 minutes, or until the turkey has turned golden.

2. Add the garlic, red and orange bell peppers, and tomatoes, then stir in the cumin seeds and paprika. Add the lemon juice and season with salt and pepper, if using. Stir well, then cover and cook, stirring from time to time, for 20 minutes, or until the tomatoes have formed a thick sauce and the turkey is cooked through and the juices run clear with no sign of pink when a piece is cut in half.

3. Meanwhile, fill a saucepan halfway with water and bring to a boil. Add the couscous and cook according to the package directions, or until just tender. Transfer to a strainer and drain well.

4. Spoon the couscous onto plates and top with the turkey stew. Mix the parsley and cilantro with the lemon zest, then sprinkle over the stew and serve.

PER SERVING: *433 cal / 6.6g fat / 0.8g sat fat / 55.5g carbs / 8.4g sugar / 9.1g fiber / 41.9g protein / 80mg sodium*

Gingered Salmon with Stir-Fried Kale

Kale, the ultimate superleaf, contains high levels of vitamins, especially vitamin C, and when paired with supernutritious salmon steaks and broccoli, it creates a delicious dish that is brimming with beneficial nutrients.

Serves 4
Prep: 20 minutes
Cook: 10 minutes

4 salmon steaks, about 5½ ounces each, skinned
2-inch piece fresh ginger, finely chopped
3 garlic cloves, finely chopped
1 red chile, seeded and finely chopped
3 tablespoons soy sauce
3 cups broccoli florets
⅓ cup water
1 tablespoon sunflower oil
1 large leek, sliced
1¾ cups thinly shredded kale
2 tablespoons Chinese rice wine
juice of 1 orange

1. Preheat the broiler to medium–high and line the bottom of the broiler pan with aluminum foil. Arrange the salmon on the broiler pan and fold up the edges of the foil to make a dish. Sprinkle with half of the ginger, half of the garlic, and half of the chile, then drizzle with 1 tablespoon of soy sauce. Broil, turning once, for 8–10 minutes, or until browned and the fish flakes easily when pressed with a knife.

2. Meanwhile, put the broccoli and water into a wok or large skillet, cover, and cook over medium–high heat for 3–4 minutes, or until the broccoli is almost tender. Pour off any remaining water.

3. Add the oil to the wok and increase the heat to high. When it is hot, add the leek, kale, and the remaining ginger, garlic, and chile and stir-fry for 2–3 minutes, or until the kale has just wilted.

4. Mix in the remaining soy sauce, the rice wine, and orange juice and cook for 1 minute more. Spoon onto plates, break up a salmon steak over each plate, and serve immediately.

PER SERVING: *416 cal / 24.1g fat / 5g sat fat / 15.3g carbs / 5.1g sugar / 2.7g fiber / 34.6g protein / 760mg sodium*

Pork-Stuffed Cabbage Leaves

Serves 4

Prep: 25 minutes
Cook: 1 hour

1 tablespoon olive oil

1 tablespoon butter

1 (14½-ounce) can diced tomatoes

2 cups chicken broth

1 onion, grated

8 large cabbage leaves,
    thick stems removed

10½ ounces fresh ground pork

½ cup freshly cooked white rice

finely grated zest of 1 lemon

2 teaspoons paprika

½ teaspoon dill seeds or caraway seeds

1 egg, lightly beaten

salt and pepper, optional

2 tablespoons chopped fresh dill,
    to garnish

Paprika and dill or caraway seeds impart a great flavor to protein-rich lean ground pork to make the tasty filling for these stuffed cabbage leaves. Serve with warm, fresh bread for a fabulous dinner.

1. Heat the oil and butter in a large skillet. Add the tomatoes, broth, and all but 2 tablespoons of the grated onion. Season with salt and pepper, if using. Bring to a boil, then reduce the heat and simmer gently while you prepare the cabbage leaves.

2. Bring a large saucepan of water to a boil. Add the cabbage leaves and blanch for 2 minutes. Drain and rinse under cold running water, then pat dry.

3. Combine the pork, rice, lemon zest, paprika, dill seeds, egg, and the remaining onion. Add salt and pepper, if using, and mix well. Divide the stuffing among the cabbage leaves. Fold over the bottom and sides of each leaf, then roll up to make a package.

4. Place the packages, seam side down, in the sauce. Cover and simmer over low heat for 45 minutes, or until cooked through.

5. Sprinkle with fresh dill and serve immediately.

PER SERVING: *369 cal / 24.8g fat / 9g sat fat / 19.7g carbs / 6.6g sugar / 4g fiber / 18.3g protein / 480mg sodium*

Slow-Cooked Beef with Mashed Lima beans

A warming and restorative casserole combining succulent shreds of fall-apart beef in a flavorful broth is served with spoonfuls of herb and garlic-seasoned lima beans, making it ideal for keeping those wintry chills at bay.

Serves 6
Prep: 30 minutes
Cook: 4¼–4¾ hours

2 tablespoons olive oil

3½ pounds beef brisket

4 onions, sliced

2 garlic cloves, crushed

1 tablespoon tomato paste

9 ripe tomatoes (about 2¼ pounds), cut into quarters

3 cups beef broth

salt and pepper, optional

2 tablespoons coarsely chopped fresh parsley, to garnish

Mashed lima beans

1 tablespoon olive oil

3 shallots, finely chopped

3 garlic cloves, finely sliced

1 fresh rosemary sprig, finely chopped

2 (15-ounce) cans lima beans, drained and rinsed

juice and zest of 1 lemon

salt and pepper, optional

1. Put a 6-quart Dutch oven or flameproof casserole dish over high heat. Add the olive oil and, using tongs to hold the meat, brown the beef all over. Set the beef aside. Reduce the heat slightly and add the onions and garlic. Cook for 4–5 minutes, or until the onion and garlic have softened. Stir in the tomato paste. Add the fresh tomatoes and continue to cook for 1–2 minutes.

2. Return the beef to the dish and nestle the beef in the center of the pot. Pour the hot broth around the beef. Season with salt and pepper, if using.

3. Reduce the heat to low. Partly cover the pot, letting just a little steam escape, and cook for 4–4 ½ hours, stirring regularly to prevent the bottom of the saucepan from sticking. Top up with a little cold water if you think the pot is looking dry. The beef should be tender and easily tear apart.

4. Meanwhile, to make the mashed lima beans, heat the oil in a large skillet and sauté the shallots, garlic, and rosemary for 3–4 minutes, or until the shallots are soft. Stir in the drained lima beans with 1 cup water. Bring to a gentle simmer and cook for 5 minutes, or until the lima beans are softened. Gently mash the lima beans, stirring through the juice and zest of the lemon. Season with salt and pepper, if using.

5. Serve the slow-cooked beef on top of a spoonful of mashed lima beans in six dishes. Garnish with the chopped parsley.

PER SERVING: *668 cal / 33.1g fat / 11g sat fat / 30.4g carbs / 9.2g sugar / 7.9g fiber / 62.9g protein / 720mg sodium*

Jerk Chicken with Papaya & Avocado Salsa

Serves 4
Prep: 35 minutes
Cook: 30–35 minutes

2¼ pounds chicken drumsticks, skinned
1 tablespoon olive oil
1 romaine lettuce, leaves separated
    and torn into pieces, optional
3 cups baby spinach, optional

Jerk spice rub

1 teaspoon allspice berries, crushed
1 teaspoon coriander seeds, crushed
1 teaspoon mild paprika
¼ teaspoon freshly grated nutmeg
1 tablespoon fresh thyme leaves
1 tablespoon black peppercorns,
    coarsely crushed
pinch of salt

Papaya & avocado salsa

1 papaya, peeled, halved, seeded,
    and cut into cubes
2 large avocados, peeled, pitted,
    and cut into cubes
finely grated zest and juice of 1 lime
½ red chile, seeded and
    finely chopped
½ red onion, finely chopped
¼ cup fresh cilantro, finely chopped
2 teaspoons chia seeds

Stimulate your senses with these sizzling spicy chicken legs, accompanied by a nutrient-rich fruit salsa and finished with a sprinkling of chia seeds. This makes a great gluten-free and dairy-free meal for sharing.

1. Preheat the oven to 400°F. To make the jerk spice rub, mix together all the ingredients in a small bowl.

2. Slash each chicken drumstick two or three times with a knife, then put them in a roasting pan and drizzle with the oil. Sprinkle the spice mix over the chicken, then rub it in with your fingers, washing your hands well afterward.

3. Roast the chicken in the preheated oven for 30–35 minutes, or until browned, with piping hot juices that run clear with no sign of pink when the tip of a knife is inserted into the thickest part of a drumstick.

4. Meanwhile, to make the salsa, put the papaya and avocados into a bowl, sprinkle with the lime zest and juice, then toss well. Add the chile, red onion, cilantro, and chia seeds and stir.

5. Toss the lettuce and spinach together, if using. Serve with the chicken and salsa.

Scallops with Pea Puree

Serves 4
Prep: 25 minutes
Cook: 12–14 minutes

3⅓ cups frozen peas

⅔ cup coarsely chopped fresh mint leaves

1¼ sticks plus 1 tablespoon butter

12 fat scallops, roes attached, if possible, and removed from their shells

salt and pepper, optional

Frozen peas and fresh scallops together pack a powerful protein punch in this tempting light lunch or dinner.

1. Bring a large saucepan of water to a boil, then add the peas. Bring back to a boil and simmer for 3 minutes. Drain the peas, then put them into a food processor or blender with the mint, 1 stick of the butter and salt, if using.

2. Process to a smooth puree, adding a little hot water if the mixture needs loosening. Cover and keep warm.

3. Pat the scallops dry, then season with salt and pepper, if using. Put a large skillet over high heat and add the remaining butter. When the butter starts to smoke, add the scallops and sear for 1–2 minutes on each side. They should be brown and crisp on the outside but light and moist in the middle. Remove the pan from the heat.

4. Spread a spoonful of pea puree on each of four plates and place three scallops on top of each. Serve immediately.

PER SERVING: *429 cal / 31.3g fat / 19.4g sat fat / 19.5g carbs / 8.1g sugar / 6.1g fiber / 19.8g protein / 520mg sodium*

Lean Beef Stir-Fry

Made in a matter of minutes, this sensational stir-fry is piled with fresh, healthy ingredients and delivers perfectly on flavor, texture, and appeal. Serve with cooked noodles or brown rice, if you desire.

Serves 2

Prep: 20 minutes
Cook: 10 minutes

2 teaspoons olive oil
5 ounces sirloin steak, visible fat removed,
    cut into thin strips
1 orange bell pepper, seeded and cut into thin strips
4 scallions, finely chopped
1–2 fresh jalapeño chiles, seeded and thinly sliced
2 garlic cloves, finely chopped
1 cup diagonally halved snow peas
4 ounces large portobello mushrooms, sliced
2 teaspoons hoisin sauce
1 tablespoon orange juice
3 cups arugula or watercress
¼ cup sweet chili sauce, to serve, optional

1. Heat the oil in a wok over medium–high heat for 30 seconds. Add the beef and stir-fry for 1 minute, or until browned. Transfer to a plate with a slotted spoon.

2. Add the orange bell pepper, scallions, jalapeño chiles, and garlic to the wok and stir-fry for 2 minutes. Add the snow peas and mushrooms and stir-fry for an additional 2 minutes.

3. Return the beef to the wok. Add the hoisin sauce and orange juice and stir-fry for 2–3 minutes, or until the beef is cooked and the vegetables are tender but still firm. Add the arugula and stir-fry until it starts to wilt. Serve immediately, with a small bowl of sweet chili sauce, if using.

PER SERVING: *359 cal / 16.4g fat / 2.6g sat fat / 34.1g carbs / 24g sugar / 5.3g fiber / 21.9g protein / 560mg sodium*

Monkfish in Pesto & Prosciutto with Ricotta Spinach

Serves 4
Prep: 30–35 minutes
Cook: 25–30 minutes

8 prosciutto slices
3 tablespoons fresh green pesto
8 large fresh basil leaves
1¼ pounds monkfish tail,
   separated into 2 fillets
1 tablespoon olive oil

Ricotta spinach

2 tablespoons olive oil
1 garlic clove, thinly sliced
5½ cups baby spinach
2 tablespoons ricotta cheese
salt and pepper, optional

Tempt your guests to the table with this sensational prosciutto and pesto-wrapped monkfish, oven-roasted to perfection and served with vitamin C-rich spinach dotted with fresh ricotta. It's certain to impress.

1. Preheat the oven to 350°F. Lay two large sheets of plastic wrap side by side on a work surface. Arrange the prosciutto slices on the plastic wrap so they lay top to bottom and the slices overlap by ½ inch. Spread the pesto all over the prosciutto, leaving a ¾-inch border around the edge. Sprinkle the basil over the top.

2. Put one monkfish fillet on top of the pesto and basil, then lay the other fillet next to it the other way around, so its thick end is against its neighbor's thin end.

3. Fold the prosciutto over the ends of the fish and then, using the plastic wrap, roll and encase the whole fillet tightly in the prosciutto. Remove the plastic wrap. Transfer to a roasting pan so the seam in the prosciutto is on the bottom, and lightly drizzle with the oil.

4. Roast in the preheated oven for 20–25 minutes, or until cooked through but still moist. Cover with aluminum foil to keep the fish warm.

5. To make the ricotta spinach, heat the oil in a large skillet over medium–high heat. Add the garlic and cook for 30 seconds, or until it is soft but not burned. Stir in the spinach and cook, stirring all the time so the oil coats the leaves, for 1 minute, or until it is wilted but not completely collapsed. Transfer to a serving bowl, dot with blobs of the ricotta, and season with salt and pepper, if using.

6. Put the fish onto a serving plate, carve into slices, and pour over any cooking juices from the roasting pan. Serve with the spinach.

PER SERVING: *372 cal / 25.1g fat / 5.7g sat fat / 2.5g carbs / 0.2g sugar / 1.1g fiber / 33.4g protein / 640mg sodium*

Lamb & Spinach Meatballs

Prep: 25–30 minutes
Cook: 1 hour

Meatballs

1 pound 2 ounces lean ground lamb
¾ cup fresh bread crumbs
½ cup frozen chopped spinach, defrosted
1 tablespoon dried oregano
1 teaspoon ground cumin
1 tablespoon olive oil, for frying

Tomato sauce

4 shallots, finely chopped
4 garlic cloves, sliced
⅔ cup fresh basil, coarsely chopped
1 tablespoon tomato paste
7 tomatoes (about 1¾ pounds), cored and coarsely chopped
⅔ cup vegetable broth
2 tablespoons red wine vinegar

14 ounces whole-wheat spaghetti
salt and pepper, optional
1 tablespoon chopped fresh basil, to garnish

Warming cumin and fragrant oregano add wonderful flavor to these succulent lamb-and-spinach meatballs. Served with a tasty tomato sauce and fiber-packed whole-wheat spaghetti, this is sure to become a family favorite.

1. To make the meatballs, put the ground lamb, bread crumbs, spinach, oregano, and cumin into a large bowl. Gently mix together using damp hands and divide the mixture into 12. Shape each portion into a round meatball.

2. Heat the olive oil in a deep skillet over medium–high heat. Add the meatballs, in batches, and cook for a few minutes, turning regularly, until browned all over. Remove from the pan and set aside.

3. To make the sauce, add the shallots and garlic to the pan and sauté in the residual oil. Add a little more oil, if needed, and sauté until the mixture is soft and beginning to caramelize. Reduce the heat to medium, stir in the basil and tomato paste, and cook for an additional minute. Stir in the chopped tomatoes and cook for 5–6 minutes, stirring until the tomatoes begin to break down.

4. Add the broth and red wine vinegar and simmer, uncovered, for 25 minutes, or until the sauce has broken down and started to thicken. Return the meatballs to the pan, cover, and cook for 12–15 minutes. Season with salt and pepper, if using.

5. Meanwhile, cook the spaghetti in boiling water for 12–14 minutes, or until tender but still firm to the bite. Drain, then divide among four bowls. Serve the meatballs and sauce over the spaghetti, garnished with fresh basil.

PER SERVING: 782 cal / 31g fat / 13.7g sat fat / 94.2g carbs / 11.2g sugar / 12g fiber / 39.9g protein / 280mg sodium

Warm Crab, Lentil & Herb Salad

Baby broccoli is an excellent source of vitamin C, and when teamed up with protein-rich lentils and crab, it creates a sensational supercharged salad that is ideal for a quick-and-easy midweek dinner for two.

Serves 2

Prep: 25 minutes
Cook: 35 minutes

7 ounces baby broccoli, any large stems cut in half
1 cup cooked green lentils
zest of 1 large lemon
3 tablespoons coarsely chopped fresh parsley
2 tablespoons coarsely chopped fresh dill
1½ cups arugula
8 ounces crabmeat
1 tablespoon coarsely chopped fresh flat-leaf parsley, to garnish
1 tablespoon coarsely chopped fresh dill, to garnish
salt and pepper, optional

Dressing

juice of 1 large lemon
2 tablespoons olive oil
3 tablespoons plain yogurt
2–3 tablespoons warm water

1. Bring a saucepan of water to a boil, reduce to a simmer, and add the broccoli. Cook for 4–5 minutes, or until the broccoli is just tender. Drain immediately under cool running water and set aside.

2. In a large bowl, gently mix the cooked broccoli, lentils, lemon zest, parsley, and dill. Season with salt and pepper, if using.

3. To make the dressing, pour the lemon juice, olive oil, and yogurt into a screw-top jar. Screw on the lid and shake vigorously. Loosen with a little warm water until you have the desired consistency.

4. Pour the dressing over the salad. Add the arugula and crabmeat and mix together delicately, being careful not to bruise the salad greens. Transfer the salad to a serving dish and garnish with the remaining dill and parsley. Serve immediately.

PER SERVING: *390 cal / 15.9g fat / 2.5g sat fat / 30.4g carbs / 5.6g sugar / 11.9g fiber / 34.3g protein / 960mg sodium*

Chicken with Pomegranate & Beet Tabbouleh

Serves 4
Prep: 25–30 minutes
Cook: 35–45 minutes

1¼ cups wheat berries

4 raw beets (about 12 ounces),
   cut into cubes

1 pound 2 ounces skinless, boneless
   chicken breasts, thinly sliced

1 small red onion, thinly sliced

1⅓ cups cherry tomatoes, halved

seeds of 1 small pomegranate

2 tablespoons coarsely chopped
   fresh mint

2½ cups baby spinach

salt and pepper, optional

Dressing
juice of 1 lemon

¼ cup virgin olive oil

2 garlic cloves, finely chopped

1 teaspoon packed light brown sugar

Piled with feel-good ingredients, beets, pomegranate seeds, and high-protein chicken create this wholesome tabbouleh.

1. Fill the bottom of a steamer halfway with water, bring to a boil, then add the wheat berries to the water. Put the beets into the steamer top, cover with a lid, and steam for 20–25 minutes, or until the wheat berries and beets are cooked. Drain the wheat berries.

2. Meanwhile, to make the dressing, put the lemon juice, oil, garlic, and sugar into a screw-top jar. Season with salt and pepper, if using, then screw on the lid and shake well.

3. Put the chicken into a bowl, add half of the dressing, and toss well. Preheat a ridged grill pan over medium–high heat. Add the chicken and cook, turning once or twice, for 8–10 minutes, or until golden and cooked all the way through. Cut one of the larger slices of chicken in half to check that the meat is no longer pink and that the juices run clear.

4. Put the red onion, tomatoes, and pomegranate seeds into a large shallow bowl. Add the wheat berries, beets, and mint. Divide the spinach among four plates, spoon the wheat berry mixture over them, then arrange the chicken on top. Serve with the remaining dressing alongside.

PER SERVING: *562 cal / 18.1g fat / 2.6g sat fat / 64.9g carbs / 12.8g sugar / 13.4g fiber / 38.2g protein / 200mg sodium*

Tuna & Wasabi Burgers

Try these tantalizing new, healthy burgers prepared with fresh tuna. They're served on toasted ciabatta, topped with nutrient-rich peppery watercress, with Japanese-inspired pickled vegetables on the side.

Serves 4

Prep: 35 minutes, plus cooling, pickling, and chilling
Cook: 20 minutes

Pickled vegetables

¼ cup rice wine vinegar

1 tablespoon packed light brown sugar

½ cup water

½ teaspoon coriander seeds, crushed

½ teaspoon mustard seeds

½ cucumber, sliced

2 carrots, cut into matchsticks

6 radishes, thinly sliced

3 shallots, thinly sliced

Tuna burgers

1 pound tuna steaks

⅓ cup finely chopped fresh cilantro

zest and juice of 1 lime

2 teaspoons wasabi paste

4 scallions, finely chopped

¼ cup mayonnaise

4 whole-wheat ciabatta slices

1 tablespoon olive oil, for brushing

1 bunch of watercress

1. To make the pickled vegetables, put the vinegar and sugar with the water into a small saucepan over high heat. Bring to a gentle simmer and stir until the sugar dissolves. Remove from the heat and add the coriander and mustard seeds. Put the cucumber, carrots, radish, and shallots into a small bowl or sterilized jar. Pour the pickling liquid over them and let cool and pickle for 4 hours or overnight.

2. Slice the tuna steaks into 1-inch pieces and briefly pulse in a food processor until just chopped. Transfer to a large bowl and combine with the cilantro, lime zest and juice, wasabi paste, scallions, and 2 tablespoons of the mayonnaise. Mix well and put into a refrigerator for 15 minutes.

3. Meanwhile, preheat a ridged grill pan. Grill the ciabatta slices until toasted and set aside.

4. Shape the tuna mixture into four patty shapes and brush each with oil. Grill for 6 minutes on each side, or until the burgers are cooked through.

5. Serve the tuna burgers on the toasted ciabatta slices, topped with the remaining mayonnaise and the watercress and with the pickled vegetables on the side.

PER SERVING: 356 cal / 10.2g fat / 1.5g sat fat / 34.4g carbs / 10.4g sugar / 4.9g fiber / 32.4g protein / 440mg sodium

Pork Medallions with Pomegranate

Vitamin-loaded kale and fresh flat-leaf parsley add vivid green to this nourishing wheat berry and pan-fried pork dish, dotted with bright pink jewel-like pomegranate seeds for extra goodness and appeal.

Serves 4
Prep: 20 minutes
Cook: 40–45 minutes

¾ cup wheat berries
¼ cup coarsely chopped fresh flat-leaf parsley
¾ cup thinly shredded kale
seeds of 1 pomegranate
1 tablespoon olive oil
1 pound 2 ounces pork medallions, visible fat removed
2 garlic cloves, finely chopped
salt and pepper, optional

Dressing
½ cup coarsely chopped walnuts
3 tablespoons virgin olive oil
1 tablespoon pomegranate molasses
juice of 1 lemon

1. Bring a medium saucepan of water to a boil. Add the wheat berries and simmer for 25–30 minutes, or until tender. Drain and rinse.

2. Meanwhile, to make the dressing, put the walnuts into a large skillet and toast for 2–3 minutes, or until just beginning to brown. Put the virgin olive oil, the pomegranate molasses, and lemon juice into a small bowl and mix together with a fork. Season with salt and pepper, if using, and stir in the hot walnuts.

3. Mix together the parsley, kale, and pomegranate seeds in a large bowl.

4. Heat the olive oil in the skillet over medium heat. Add the pork and garlic, season with salt and pepper, if using, and cook for 10 minutes, turning halfway through, until browned and cooked. Cut into the center of one of the pork medallions; any juices that run out should be clear and piping hot with steam rising. Slice the pork into strips.

5. Add the wheat berries to the kale mixture and gently toss. Transfer to a serving plate, pour the dressing over the mixture, then top with the pork.

PER SERVING: *518 cal / 25.3g fat / 3.5g sat fat / 41.6g carbs / 5.2g sugar / 8.3g fiber / 34.3g protein / 320mg sodium*

Country-Style Ham & Pinto Beans

Pinto beans are an excellent low-fat source of protein, fiber, and other essential nutrients and combine perfectly with fresh vegetables and cooked ham to make this satisfying, soul-warming dinnertime dish.

Serves 4
Prep: 15–20 minutes
Cook: 1 hour

2 tablespoons olive oil

1 large onion, chopped

2 green bell peppers, seeded and chopped

4 garlic cloves, crushed

1 teaspoon ground cumin

3 cups cooked pinto beans

3 tablespoons ketchup

2 tablespoons packed dark brown sugar

2 tablespoons apple cider vinegar

2 teaspoons Worcestershire sauce

2 teaspoons French mustard

⅔ cup chicken broth

1¾ cups cubed cooked ham

salt and pepper, optional

2 tablespoons chopped fresh flat-leaf parsley, to garnish

2 cups freshly cooked brown rice, to serve

1. Heat the oil in a Dutch oven or flameproof casserole dish set over medium–low heat. Add the onion and bell peppers and cook for 5 minutes, stirring occasionally. Add the garlic and cumin, stir to combine, and cook for an additional minute.

2. Add the beans, ketchup, sugar, vinegar, Worcestershire sauce, mustard, broth, and ham, stirring to combine everything well. Bring to a simmer, cover with a lid, and cook gently for 45 minutes.

3. Season with salt and pepper, if using, and sprinkle with the parsley. Serve with freshly cooked brown rice.

PER SERVING: 503 cal / 11.7g fat / 2.3g sat fat / 72.1g carbs / 12.9g sugar / 14.5g fiber / 29.6g protein / 920mg sodium

236

Red Cabbage, Turkey & Quinoa Pilaf

Quinoa, which is a seed and not a grain, is a healthy low-carb alternative to rice and is high in protein, too. It pairs up perfectly with red cabbage and low-fat turkey in this sustaining dinnertime dish.

Serves 4

Prep: 25 minutes, plus standing
Cook: 50–55 minutes

½ cup white quinoa
½ cup red quinoa
¼ cup vegetable oil
1 large red onion, halved and sliced
1 teaspoon cumin seeds, crushed
4-inch cinnamon stick, broken
½ head of red cabbage, core removed, leaves sliced into ribbons
1½ cups chicken broth
2½ cups bite-size cooked turkey pieces
2 carrots, shaved into ribbons
½ cup dried cranberries
⅔ cup Brazil nuts, coarsely chopped
salt and pepper, optional
2 tablespoons fresh flat-leaf parsley leaves, to garnish

1. Put the white quinoa and red quinoa into a strainer and rinse under cold running water, then put the grains into a saucepan with salt, if using, and enough water to cover by ½ inch. Bring to a boil, cover, and simmer over low heat for 15 minutes, or according to the package directions. Remove from the heat but keep the pan covered for 5 minutes to let the grains to swell. Fluff up the grains with a fork and set aside.

2. Heat the oil in a large skillet over medium–high heat. Add the onion with the spices and sauté for 5 minutes, or until the onion is soft but not browned.

3. Add the cabbage and 1 cup of the broth, then season with salt and pepper, if using. Cover and cook over medium heat for 15–20 minutes, until the cabbage is just tender. Add the turkey, carrots, cranberries, and Brazil nuts. Cook, uncovered, for 5 minutes, until the turkey is heated through.

4. Gently stir in the cooked quinoa. Add the remaining broth and check the seasoning, if using. Cook for 2 minutes to heat through. Garnish with parsley and serve immediately.

PER SERVING: *688 cal* / *32.2g fat* / *6g sat fat* / *67.3g carbs* / *22.6g sugar* / *11.1g fiber* / *38.4g protein* / *400mg sodium*

The Sweet Stuff

Healthy Apple Crisp

Serves 6

Serves 6

Prep: 25 minutes, plus cooling
Cook: 40–45 minutes

5 cooking apples (about 1¾ pounds),
    such as Granny Smiths, peeled, cored,
    and chopped into ¾-inch chunks
pinch of ground cloves
pinch of ground cinnamon
1 teaspoon ground ginger
3 tablespoons packed brown sugar

Topping

2⅓ cups rolled oats
½ teaspoon ground cinnamon
3 tablespoons honey
3 tablespoons coconut oil,
    at room temperature
⅓ cup coarsely chopped
    macadamia nuts
2 tablespoons raw brown sugar

Although the sugar content of this fruity family favorite has been reduced, it still tastes just as good. Healthy whole-grain oats, macadamia nuts, and coconut oil add extra goodness to the wholesome topping, too.

1. Preheat the oven to 350°F.

2. Put the apple chunks into a large saucepan. Add 2 tablespoons of cold water, the cloves, cinnamon, ginger, and brown sugar and put over medium heat. Stew for about 15 minutes, stirring regularly, or until the apples begin to just lose their shape. Once mushy, put the apples into a 1¼-quart baking dish.

3. To make the topping, simply put the oats into a medium bowl, then stir in the cinnamon, honey, coconut oil, macadamia nuts, and sugar and mix well.

4. Sprinkle the topping mixture over the stewed apple and bake for 25–30 minutes, or until golden. Remove from the oven and let cool for a few minutes before serving.

PER SERVING: *378 cal / 15.4g fat / 7.3g sat fat / 59g carbs / 32.4g sugar / 5.7g fiber / 5.4g protein / trace sodium*

Green Tea Fruit Salad

Bursting with beneficial vitamins and antioxidants, this multicolored fruit salad provides a light and delicious dessert. Pistachios and pomegranate seeds add a final flourish of goodness, too.

Serves 4

Prep: 25 minutes, plus brewing, cooling, and chilling
Cook: No cooking

2 teaspoons loose green tea
1 cup boiling water
1 tablespoon honey
½ small watermelon, cut into cubes
1 large mango, cut into cubes
1 papaya, seeded, cut into cubes
2 pears, cut into cubes
2 kiwis, cut into cubes
2 tablespoons coarsely chopped fresh mint
seeds of ½ pomegranate
2 tablespoons coarsely chopped pistachio nuts

1. Put the tea into a teapot or heatproof bowl, pour the boiling water over the leaves, and let brew for 3–4 minutes. Strain into a small heatproof bowl, stir in the honey, and let cool.

2. Put the watermelon, mango, and papaya into a large serving bowl, then add the pears, kiwis, and mint. Pour the cooled green tea over the fruits and stir everything gently together.

3. Cover the fruit salad with plastic wrap and chill in the refrigerator for 1 hour. Stir gently to mix the tea through the fruit.

4. Spoon the fruit salad into four bowls. Serve immediately, sprinkled with the pomegranate seeds and pistachio nuts.

PER SERVING: *258 cal / 3.5g fat / 0.4g sat fat / 59.5g carbs / 45.3g sugar / 8.4g fiber / 4.1g protein / trace sodium*

Coconut Milk, Strawberry & Honey Ice Cream

Serves 6

Prep: 30 minutes, plus freezing
Cook: No cooking

*1 pound strawberries,
  hulled and halved*
1¾ cups coconut milk
⅓ cup honey
*3 tablespoons crushed hazelnuts,
  to serve*

Fresh strawberries, filled with healthy vitamin C, combine wonderfullly with coconut milk and healthful honey to produce a really sumptuous homemade ice cream. Crushed hazelnuts add a final feel-good crunch for serving.

1. Puree the strawberries in a food processor or blender, then press through a strainer set over a mixing bowl to remove the seeds.

2. Add the coconut milk and honey to the strawberry puree and whisk together.

3. Pour the mixture into a large roasting pan until it is a depth of ¾ inch. Cover the top of the pan with plastic wrap, then freeze for about 2 hours, until just set.

4. Scoop back into the food processor or blender and process again until smooth to break down the ice crystals. Pour into a plastic container or 9 x 5 x 3-inch loaf pan lined with nonstick parchment paper. Place the lid on the plastic container or fold the paper over the ice cream in the loaf pan. Return to the freezer for 3–4 hours, or until firm enough to scoop.

5. Serve immediately or keep in the freezer overnight or until needed. Thaw at room temperature for 15 minutes to soften slightly, then scoop into individual dishes and top with crushed hazelnuts to serve.

PER SERVING: *230 cal / 17.5g fat / 12.8g sat fat / 20.1g carbs / 17.1g sugar / 2g fiber / 2.6g protein / trace sodium*

Black Bean & Date Brownies

Black beans and Medjool dates enrich these hard-to-resist brownies to create a delicious power snack that will be perfect when you need a chocolate hit or simply crave something sweet after a meal.

Makes 16

Prep: 25 minutes, plus cooling
Cook: 28 minutes, plus standing

½ cup plus 1 tablespoon bittersweet chocolate chips
3 tablespoons coconut oil
1½ cups drained and rinsed black beans in water
7 Medjool dates (about 6 ounces), halved and pitted
3 eggs
⅓ cup firmly packed light brown sugar
1 teaspoon vanilla extract
⅔ cup unsweetened cocoa powder
1½ teaspoons baking powder
½ teaspoon ground cinnamon
¼ teaspoon sea salt

1. Preheat the oven to 350°F. Line a shallow 8-inch square cake pan with a square of nonstick parchment paper.

2. Add ⅓ cup of the chocolate chips to a small saucepan with the oil and heat over low heat until the oil has melted. Remove from the heat and let stand for a few minutes, until the chocolate has melted completely.

3. Meanwhile, add the beans and dates to a food processor or blender and process to a coarse puree. Add the eggs, sugar, vanilla extract, and chocolate-and-oil-mixture, and process again until smooth.

4. Mix together the cocoa powder, baking powder, cinnamon, and salt, then add to the bean mixture and process briefly until smooth.

5. Spoon into the prepared pan and spread in an even layer. Bake in the preheated oven for about 25 minutes, or until the cake is well risen, beginning to crack around the edges and still slightly soft in the center.

6. Sprinkle with the remaining chocolate chips and let cool for 20 minutes. Lift the paper and brownies out of the pan and transfer to a wire rack to cool completely. Cut into 16 small pieces, lift off the paper, and serve or store in an airtight container for up to two days.

PER BROWNIE: 227 cal / 10.8g fat / 6.9g sat fat / 30g carbs / 21g sugar / 6.5g fiber / 5.7g protein / 200mg sodium

Tofu Lemon Cheesecake

Serves 10
Prep: 30–35 minutes, plus chilling
Cook: 5 minutes

Cheesecake

1 cup pecans
7 soft dried dates (about 6 ounces)
12 gingersnaps
2 tablespoons agave syrup

Filling

12 ounces firm silken tofu
1¼ cups cream cheese
½ cup Greek-style plain yogurt
juice and grated zest of 3 lemons,
    plus 1 tablespoon zest to decorate
½ cup firmly packed light brown sugar
½ teaspoon vanilla extract
2 tablespoons powdered gelatin
    (two ¼-ounces envelopes)
⅓ cup cold water

Fiber-filled dates and naturally sweet agave syrup add flavor and appeal to the crunchy ginger cookie crust, and zesty lemons add the finest refreshing flavor to the topping of this tasty, chilled cheesecake.

1. Line an 8-inch round springform baking pan with parchment paper.

2. To make the crust, put the pecans, dates, gingersnaps, and agave syrup into a food processor and pulse until the mixture comes together. The mixture should be slightly sticky when rolled in your hands. Put the mixture into the bottom of your prepared pan and press down to create an even crust.

3. To make the filling, drain any excess water from the tofu and put into a food processor with the cream cheese, yogurt, lemon juice, lemon zest, brown sugar, and vanilla extract. Blend until silky smooth.

4. Put the powdered gelatin into a small heatproof bowl and pour the cold water over it. Set the bowl over a saucepan of gently simmering water. Stir the gelatin until it has dissolved into the liquid and, working quickly, pour the liquid gelatin into the tofu mixture. Blend the filling again until the gelatin is fully incorporated.

5. Spoon the filling on top of the crust and place in the refrigerator to chill for 6 hours or overnight. Serve in slices, decorated with lemon zest.

PER SERVING: *368 cal / 22.2g fat / 7.7g sat fat / 37.6g carbs / 29.7g sugar / 2.9g fiber / 8.4g protein / 160mg sodium*

Avocado Chocolate Mousse

Low in sugar, high in heart-friendly monounsaturated fat, and suitable for vegetarians, this gorgeous, silken mousse is served in small portions, because each spoonful packs a powerful creamy chocolate flavor.

Serves 4
Prep: 20 minutes
Cook: No cooking

2 ripe avocados, coarsely chopped
⅓ cup unsweetened cocoa powder
2 tablespoons rice malt syrup
1 teaspoon vanilla extract
pinch of sea salt
2 tablespoons unsweetened almond milk

1. Put all the ingredients into a blender or food processor and process until combined. Scrape down the sides and process for an additional minute, or until the mousse is airy. If it is still too thick, add a splash more almond milk and process again briefly.

2. Spoon the mousse into small teacups or serving dishes and serve immediately. Alternatively, you can cover and chill the mousses in the refrigerator for up to 4 hours.

Skinny Banana Split Sundaes

Serves 2

Prep: 20 minutes,
  plus freezing and cooling
Cook: 8–10 minutes

2 small bananas, coarsely chopped
6 unblanched almonds,
  coarsely chopped

Chocolate sauce

2 tablespoons packed light brown sugar
3 tablespoons unsweetened
  cocoa powder
⅓ cup low-fat milk
1 ounce bittersweet chocolate, chopped
½ teaspoon vanilla extract

There's nothing childish about these reduced-fat desserts. The naturally sweet ripe bananas are low in fat and rich in vitamins, minerals, and fiber, so they produce the perfect frozen ice to accompany a sumptuous chocolate sauce.

1. Put the bananas into a plastic container and freeze for 2 hours. Transfer to a food processor and process until smooth and creamy. Return to the container, replace the lid, and freeze for 1 hour, or until firm.

2. To make the chocolate sauce, put the sugar, cocoa powder, and milk into a small saucepan and bring to a simmer over medium heat. Reduce the heat to low and cook, stirring constantly, for about 1 minute, or until the sugar and cocoa powder have dissolved.

3. Remove from the heat, then stir in the chocolate until it has melted. Stir in the vanilla extract. Let the mixture cool slightly.

4. Place a dry skillet over high heat. Add the almonds, cover, and dry-fry for 3–4 minutes, or until toasted.

5. Scoop the banana puree into two glasses or bowls, drizzle with the warm chocolate sauce, and sprinkle with the almonds.

Chia Seed & Banana Ice Pops

Chia seeds are a nutritional treasure trove, rich in omega-3 fatty acids and a good source of vitamins, minerals, protein, and fiber. Combined with bananas, honey, and yogurt, they create these sensational full-of-goodness ice pops.

Makes 6
Prep: 20 minutes, plus freezing
Cook: No cooking

3 large, ripe bananas
3 tablespoons Greek-style plain yogurt
2 teaspoons honey
2 teaspoons chia seeds

You will also need:
6 (¼-cup) ice pop molds
6 ice pop sticks

1. Blend the bananas, Greek yogurt, and honey in a blender or food processor until you have a thick, smooth consistency. Stir in the chia seeds.

2. Transfer the mixture to a small bowl and pour the mixture evenly into the six ice pop molds.

3. Place an ice pop stick in the center of each mold. Place in the freezer and let freeze for 6 hours before serving.

4. To unmold the ice pops, dip the frozen molds into warm water for a few seconds and gently release the ice pops while holding the sticks.

PER ICE POP: *84 cal / 1.2g fat / 0.5g sat fat / 18.5g carbs / 10.6g sugar / 2.3g fiber / 1.9g protein / trace sodium*

Chai Tea Cookies

Makes 30
Prep: 25–30 minutes,
 plus chilling and cooling
Cook: 18–20 minutes

½ cup packed light brown sugar
2 tablespoons dry loose chai tea
 (about 4 teabags)
¼ teaspoon salt
1 cup whole-wheat flour
1 teaspoon vanilla extract
1 stick cold, unsalted butter
2 tablespoons whole-wheat flour,
 for dusting

Spicy, pungent, antioxidant-rich chai tea adds delicious flavor to these fiber-filled cookies, which provide a healthy, crunchy treat when you crave something sweet. They keep well for a few days, too.

1. Preheat the oven to 350°F and line a baking sheet with parchment paper.

2. Put the brown sugar, tea, and salt into a food processor and process until the tea has been ground to a fine powder. Add the flour, vanilla extract, and butter and process until well combined and the mixture begins to hold together. If the mixture is too dry, add cold water, ½ teaspoon at a time, and process until the mixture just comes together.

3. Turn out the dough onto a sheet of plastic wrap and shape into a log. Wrap tightly and refrigerate for 15 minutes.

4. Roll out the dough on a lightly floured surface to about ⅛–inch thick and cut into circles, using a round 2½-inch cookie cutter (or use the shape of your choice). Transfer the cookies to the prepared baking sheet and bake in the preheated oven for 18–20 minutes, or until they begin to turn golden at the edges.

5. Remove from the oven and transfer the cookies to a wire rack to cool completely.

PER COOKIE: *58 cal / 3.2g fat / 2g sat fat / 7g carbs / 3.3g sugar / 0.5g fiber / 0.7g protein / trace sodium*

Coconut & Mango Quinoa Puddings

Serves 4

Prep: 20 minutes,
  plus standing and cooling
Cook: 15–20 minutes

1 ¼ cups coconut milk

⅔ cup quinoa, rinsed

2 cups coarsely chopped mango

⅓ cup superfine or granulated sugar

juice of 1 large lime

1 ½-inch piece fresh ginger,
  cut into chunks

⅔ cup blueberries

¼ cup toasted dried coconut shavings

Enjoy the fragrant flavors of this dairy-free dessert and benefit from the antioxidant goodness of fresh mango and blueberries.

1. Put the coconut milk and quinoa into a small saucepan and bring to a boil over high heat. Reduce the heat to low, cover, and simmer for 10–15 minutes, or according to the package directions, until most of the liquid has evaporated. Remove from the heat and set aside for 7 minutes to let the grains swell. Fluff up with a fork, put into a bowl, and let cool.

2. Meanwhile, put the mango, sugar, and lime juice into a food processor. Squeeze the ginger through a garlic press and add the juice to the food processor. Process for 30 seconds, or until you have a smooth puree.

3. Mix the mango puree into the cooled quinoa, then cover and let stand for 30 minutes.

4. Spoon the dessert into four small bowls and sprinkle with the blueberries and coconut shavings. Serve immediately.

PER SERVING: *425 cal / 20.4g fat / 16.4g sat fat / 59.5g carbs / 35.5g sugar / 4.7g fiber / 6.8g protein / trace sodium*

Mocha Soufflés with Mascarpone

You don't need to skimp on dessert with these luscious low-sugar soufflés. Crammed with vitamins, minerals, and heart-healthy monounsaturated fat, ground almonds add goodness to these tempting baked desserts.

Serves 4

Prep: 25–30 minutes, plus cooling
Cook: 18–20 minutes

2 teaspoons butter, to grease

2 tablespoons ground almonds

1 tablespoon unsweetened cocoa powder

1 tablespoon prepared strong espresso

pinch of sea salt

⅓ cup cold water

3 egg whites

1 tablespoon rice malt syrup

1 teaspoon unsweetened cocoa powder, to dust

¼ cup mascarpone cheese, to serve

1. Preheat the oven to 375°F. Lightly grease four ramekins (individual ceramic dishes), then sprinkle with the ground almonds. Roll and rotate the ramekins so the almonds stick to the butter, coating all sides.

2. Put the cocoa powder, espresso, salt, and water into a small saucepan and cook, stirring over low heat, until smooth. Increase the heat to medium–high and bring to a boil, then cook for an additional 1 minute. Pour the mixture into a large bowl and let cool.

3. Put the egg whites in a separate large, clean grease-free bowl and whisk until they form soft peaks. Add the rice malt syrup and whisk again until you have stiff peaks. Using a metal spoon, gently fold a spoonful of the egg white into the cocoa mixture, preserving as much air as possible, then fold in the rest.

4. Spoon the mixture into the prepared ramekins. Bake for 10–12 minutes, or until the soufflés are towering out of the ramekins.

5. Add a tablespoon of mascarpone to each ramekin and sprinkle with cocoa powder. Serve immediately, before the soufflés start to collapse.

PER SERVING: *156 cal / 12g fat / 7.5g sat fat / 8.7g carbs / 5.4g sugar / 0.8g fiber / 4.4g protein / 200mg sodium*

Spiced Apple Whole-Wheat Cupcakes

Makes 12
Prep: 35–40 minutes, plus cooling
Cook: 50 minutes–1¼ hours

3 crisp sweet apples,
   such as Pippin or Cortland
finely grated zest and juice of 1 lemon
¾ cup whole-wheat all-purpose flour
½ cup brown rice flour
2 teaspoons baking powder
½ teaspoon ground allspice
1 stick unsalted butter,
   softened and diced
½ cup firmly packed light brown sugar
2 eggs, beaten
1 cup crème fraîche or
   Greek-style plain yogurt
¼ teaspoon ground allspice, to decorate

For a healthy sweet snack during the day or after a meal, opt for these appealing whole-wheat apple cupcakes that are topped with lightly spiced crème fraîche and finished with a flurry of baked apple slices.

1. To make the applesauce, peel, core, and coarsely chop two of the apples, then put them into a saucepan. Add the lemon zest and half of the juice. Cover and cook over low heat for 5–10 minutes, or until soft. Mash until smooth, then let cool. Preheat the oven to 350°F.

2. Put 12 paper liners or squares of parchment paper in a 12-cup muffin pan. Put the whole-wheat and rice flours, baking powder, and allspice into a small bowl and mix well.

3. Cream the butter and sugar together in a large bowl. Beat in alternate spoonfuls of the eggs and the flour mixture until it is all used, then stir in ⅔ cup of the applesauce (reserve any remaining for another time).

4. Spoon the batter evenly into the paper liners. Bake for 15–18 minutes, or until well risen and the tops spring back when pressed with a fingertip. Let cool for 5 minutes, then transfer to a wire rack to cool completely.

5. Line a baking sheet with parchment paper. Put the rest of the lemon juice in a medium bowl. Thinly slice the remaining apple, toss it in the lemon juice, then arrange it on the prepared baking sheet. Reduce the oven temperature to 225°F and cook the apple slices, turning once, for 30–45 minutes, or until just beginning to brown. Turn off the oven and leave the apples to cool inside it. Lift the slices with a spatula and cut them in half.

6. Top each cupcake with a spoonful of crème fraîche, sprinkle with allspice, and put two apple slice halves on top.

PER CUPCAKE: 244 cal / 14.8g fat / 9.3g sat fat / 26.1g carbs / 14g sugar / 17g fiber / 3.1g protein / 80mg sodium

Gluten & Dairy-Free Orange & Almond Cake

Serves 8

Prep: 30 minutes, plus cooling
Cook: 2 hours 35 minutes–
    3 hours 5 minutes

2 small oranges
2 teaspoons olive oil, to grease
6 eggs
1 cup firmly packed brown sugar
2½ cups ground almonds (almond meal)
1 teaspoon gluten-free baking powder
½ teaspoon ground cloves

Fig topping

4 plump fresh figs, cut into wedges
⅓ cup sliced almonds, toasted
zest of 1 orange

A real sweet treat for those following a gluten- or dairy-free diet, this deliciously moist cake is packed with nourishing ground almonds and juicy fresh oranges, then served with a fabulous fig topping.

1. Put the oranges into a large saucepan with some cold water. Bring to a gentle simmer and cook for 1½–2 hours. Drain and, when cool, cut each orange in half and remove the seeds. Put the oranges—skins, pith, fruit, and all—into a blender or food processor and process.

2. Preheat the oven to 375°F. Grease and line an 8-inch round springform cake pan.

3. Put the eggs into a mixing bowl and gently beat them with a whisk. Add the sugar, almonds, baking powder, and ground cloves to the bowl. Mix well before stirring in the pulped oranges.

4. Pour the batter into the prepared pan and bake for 1 hour in the preheated oven, or until golden and a toothpick inserted in the center comes out clean. Remove from the oven and let cool in the pan on a wire rack. Once the cake is completely cool, remove from the pan.

5. Decorate the cake with the figs, toasted almonds, and fresh orange zest.

PER SERVING: 409 cal / 23.3g fat / 2.8g sat fat / 42.4g carbs / 35.3g sugar / 4.9g fiber / 12.7g protein / 120mg sodium

Fruity Ice Pops

Fresh mango and strawberries, filled with healthy vitamins, add wonderful color and flavor to these easy-to-make iced yogurt treats. Sweetened naturally with honey, these low-fat ice pops can be enjoyed by all the family.

Makes 8

Prep: 30 minutes, plus freezing
Cook: No cooking

2 cups diced mango
½ cup plus 1 tablespoon honey
1¼ cups plain yogurt
2 teaspoons vanilla extract
10½ ounces strawberries, hulled (about 2 cups prepared)

You will also need:

8 (½-cup) ice pop molds
8 ice pop sticks

1. Put the mango into a blender or food processor and process to a puree. Transfer to a small bowl, add 3 tablespoons of the honey, and stir well.

2. Pour the mixture into 8 (½-cup) ice pop molds. Freeze for 2 hours, or until firm.

3. When the mango mixture is frozen, put the yogurt, vanilla extract, and 3 tablespoons of honey into a bowl and stir well. Spoon the mixture over the frozen mango mixture. Insert the ice pop sticks and freeze for 2–3 hours, or until firm.

4. When the vanilla mixture is frozen, put the strawberries and remaining 3 tablespoons of honey into a blender and process to a puree. Strain out the seeds using a fine metal strainer. Pour the strawberry puree over the frozen vanilla mixture and freeze for 2–3 hours, or until firm.

5. To unmold the ice pops, dip the frozen molds into warm water for a few seconds and gently release the ice pops while holding the sticks.

PER ICE POP: *134 cal / 1.5g fat / 0.8g sat fat / 30.3g carbs / 28.7g sugar / 1.4g fiber / 2g protein / trace sodium*

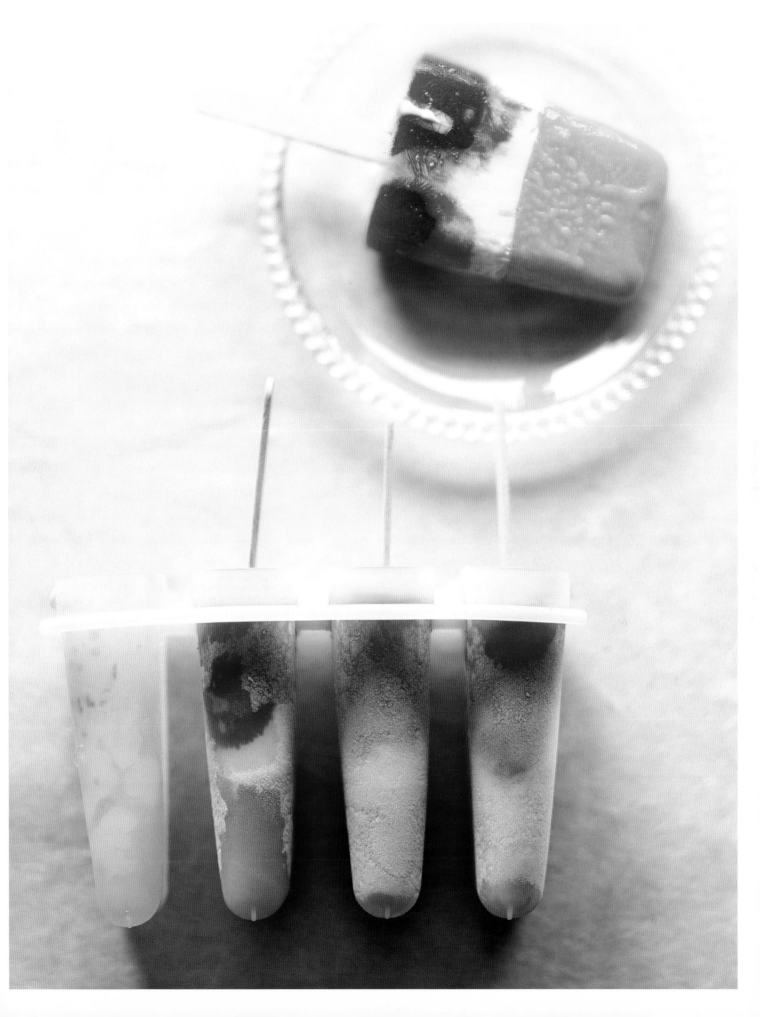

Mixed Berry Yellow Cakes

Light and airy low-fat yellow cakes are topped with thick plain yogurt and a medley of mixed berries bursting with antioxidants, to create these delightful individual desserts, great for a gathering of family or friends.

Makes 6

Prep: 30 minutes, plus cooling
Cook: 12–15 minutes

1 tablespoon olive oil, to grease
3 eggs
⅓ cup superfine or granulated sugar
½ teaspoon vanilla extract
½ cup brown rice flour
1 cup low-fat Greek-style plain yogurt
1¼ cups raspberries
1 cup hulled and sliced strawberries
⅔ cup blueberries
1 tablespoon confectioners' sugar, sifted

1. Preheat the oven to 350°F. Brush six ¾-cup tube mold pans with a little oil and put them on a baking sheet.

2. Put the eggs, superfine sugar, and vanilla extract into a large bowl and beat with an electric handheld mixer for 5 minutes, or until the mixture is thick and leaves a trail when the beaters are lifted.

3. Sift the flour over the egg mixture, then gently fold it in with a large metal spoon. Spoon the batter into the pans and ease it into an even layer, being careful not to knock out any air.

4. Bake in the preheated oven for 12–15 minutes, or until the cakes are risen and golden brown and beginning to shrink away from the edges.

5. Let cool in the pans for 5 minutes. Loosen the edges of the cakes with a blunt knife and turn them out onto a wire rack. Let cool completely.

6. Put the cakes on serving plates, spoon the yogurt into the center, then pile the fruits on top. Dust with sifted confectioners' sugar and serve immediately.

PER CAKE: *222 cal / 5.3g fat / 1.2g sat fat / 35.5g carbs / 21.4g sugar / 3.2g fiber / 9g protein / 40mg sodium*

Raspberry & Watermelon Sorbet

Both refreshing and palate-cleansing, this fabulous fat-free fruit sorbet makes a great light dessert. Fresh raspberries and juicy watermelon make it jam-packed with health-enhancing vitamins and minerals, especially vitamin C.

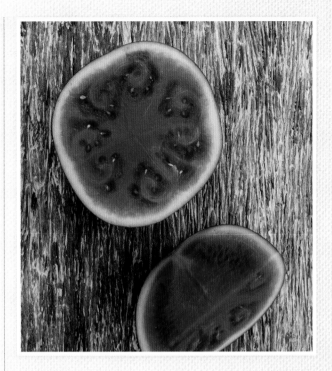

Serves 4

Prep: 30 minutes, plus cooling and freezing
Cook: 7–9 minutes

½ cup superfine or granulated sugar
⅔ cup cold water
finely grated zest and juice of 1 lime
1¾ cups raspberries
1 small watermelon, cut into chunks
1 egg white

1. Put the sugar, water, and lime zest into a small saucepan and cook over low heat, stirring, until the sugar has dissolved. Increase to high until the mixture comes to a boil, then reduce the heat to medium and simmer gently for 3–4 minutes. Let the lime syrup cool completely.

2. Put the raspberries and watermelon into a food processor, in batches, and process to a puree. Press the mixture through a strainer into a bowl to remove any remaining seeds.

3. Put the puree into a loaf pan, pour in the lime syrup through a strainer, then stir in the lime juice. Freeze for 3–4 hours, or until the sorbet is beginning to freeze around the edges and the center is still mushy.

4. Transfer the sorbet to a food processor and process to break up the ice crystals. Put the egg white in a small bowl and lightly whisk with a fork until frothy, then mix it into the sorbet.

5. Pour the sorbet into a plastic or metal container, cover, and freeze for 3–4 hours, or until firm. Let soften at room temperature for 10–15 minutes before serving. Eat within a week of freezing.

PER SERVING: *232 cal / 0.8g fat / 0g sat fat / 57.7g carbs / 48.8g sugar / 4.9g fiber / 3.3g protein / trace sodium*

Coconut, Cacao & Hazelnut Truffles

Makes 20
Prep: 25 minutes, plus storing
Cook: No cooking

⅔ cup unblanched hazelnuts
½ cup cacao nibs
6 dried soft figs, coarsely chopped
⅓ cup dry unsweetened coconut
1 tablespoon maple syrup
finely grated zest and juice of
    ½ small orange
1 tablespoon finely chopped cacao nibs,
    for coating
2 tablespoons dry unsweetened
    coconut, for coating

This supercharged and tasty power snack is crammed with natural ingredients, creating the perfect energy-giving pick-me-up.

1. Add the hazelnuts and the cacao nibs to a food processor and process until finely chopped.

2. Add the figs, coconut, maple syrup, and orange zest and juice to the processor, and process until finely chopped and the mixture has come together in a ball.

3. Scoop the mixture out of the food processor, then cut into 20 even pieces. Roll into small balls between the palms of your hands.

4. Mix the chopped cacao nibs with the coconut on a sheet of nonstick parchment paper or a plate. Roll the truffles, one at a time, in the cacao-and-coconut mixture, then arrange in a small plastic container. Store in the refrigerator for up to three days.

PER TRUFFLE: *63 cal / 5g fat / 1.9g sat fat / 4.9g carbs / 2.6g sugar / 2g fiber / 1.3g protein / trace sodium*

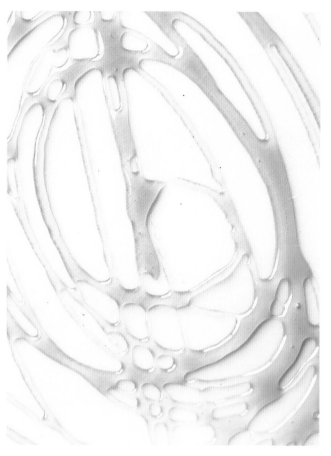

Chocolate & Chia Puddings

Coconut milk and plain yogurt add an appealing creaminess to these chilled chocolate puddings, plus agave syrup sweetens them naturally and chia seeds add that extra nutrient boost.

Serves 3

Prep: 20 minutes, plus chilling
Cook: No cooking

2 tablespoons unsweetened cocoa powder
2 tablespoons agave syrup
⅓ cup coconut milk
½ cup Greek-style plain yogurt
2 tablespoons chia seeds
1 teaspoon vanilla extract
1 kiwi, sliced, to decorate
1¾ ounces semisweet chocolate, coarsely chopped, to decorate

1. Put the cocoa powder and agave syrup into a large bowl and mix well to remove any lumps. Stir in the coconut milk, Greek yogurt, chia seeds, and vanilla extract and mix thoroughly.

2. Cover and refrigerate for 4–6 hours. Remove the mixture from the refrigerator; it should be thick at this stage. Using an electric handheld mixer, process the mixture until smooth, then carefully divide among three small dessert glasses.

3. Chill the puddings for an additional hour. Decorate with the kiwi slices and semisweet chocolate and serve.

PER SERVING: *307 cal / 18.8g fat / 11.8g sat fat / 29.4g carbs / 18.7g sugar / 7g fiber / 7.9g protein / trace sodium*

Celebration Chocolate & Beet Cake

Serves 8
Prep: 35–40 minutes, plus cooling
Cook: 1½ hours

½ tablespoon unsalted butter,
　for greasing
2 raw beets, cut into cubes
5½ ounces bittersweet chocolate,
　broken into pieces
⅓ cup unsweetened cocoa powder
2 teaspoons baking powder
1 cup whole-wheat flour
⅛ cup brown rice flour
1¾ sticks unsalted butter,
　softened and diced
1 cup firmly packed light brown sugar
4 eggs
2 tablespoons milk
1¼ cups heavy cream

Fresh beets add delicious natural sweetness to this indulgent chocolate cake and keep it wonderfully moist, too. This special occasion whole-wheat cake will soon become the all-time favorite for all committed chocoholics.

1. Preheat the oven to 325°F. Lightly grease an 8-inch round springform cake pan and line with parchment paper.

2. Fill the bottom of a steamer halfway with water, bring to a boil, then put the beets into the steamer top. Cover with a lid and steam for 15 minutes, or until tender. Transfer the beets to a food processor and add ¼ cup of water from the bottom of the steamer. Puree until smooth, then let cool.

3. Put 4 ounces of the chocolate into a heatproof bowl set over a saucepan of gently simmering water, making sure the bowl doesn't touch the water. Let stand for 5 minutes, or until the chocolate has melted.

4. Sift the cocoa into a second bowl, then stir in the baking powder and whole-wheat and rice flours.

5. Cream the butter and ¾ cup of the sugar together in a large bowl. Beat in the eggs, one by one, adding spoonfuls of the flour mixture between each egg and beating well after each addition.

Stir in the remaining flour mixture, the pureed beets, and melted chocolate, beat until smooth, then mix in enough of the milk to make a soft dropping consistency.

6. Spoon the batter into the prepared pan and spread it into an even layer. Bake for 1 hour, or until well risen, the top is slightly cracked, and a toothpick comes out cleanly when inserted into the center of the cake. Let cool for 15 minutes, then remove from the pan, peel off the parchment paper, and transfer the cake to a wire rack.

7. To finish, melt the remaining chocolate in a heatproof bowl set over a saucepan of gently simmering water, making sure the bowl doesn't touch the water. Put the cream in a bowl, add the remaining sugar, and whisk until soft swirls form. Cut the cake in half and put the bottom half on a serving plate. Spoon one-third of the cream mixture onto the bottom of the cake, add the top half of the cake, then spoon the remaining cream on the top. Drizzle with the melted chocolate and serve.

PER SERVING: *662 cal / 46.6g fat / 27.9g sat fat / 56.5g carbs / 32.8g sugar / 5.6g fiber / 9.2g protein / 200mg sodium*

Passion Fruit & Strawberry Yogurts

Passion fruit and strawberries add vibrant color and vital vitamins to these zesty single-serving yogurt desserts. Each one is finished with a sprinkling of nutrient-rich, dried goji berries for an additional nutritious lift.

Serves 4
Prep: 20–25 minutes, plus cooling and chilling
Cook: 2–3 minutes

¼ cup dry unsweetened coconut

7 ounces strawberries, hulled

finely grated zest and juice of 1 lime

1½ cups low-fat Greek-style plain yogurt

4 teaspoons honey

2 passion fruit, halved

1 tablespoon coarsely chopped dried goji berries

1. Add the coconut to a dry skillet and cook over medium heat for 2–3 minutes, shaking the pan, until light golden. Remove the coconut from the heat and let cool.

2. Coarsely mash the strawberries and mix with half of the lime juice.

3. Add the lime zest, remaining lime juice, the yogurt, and honey to a bowl and stir together. Add three-quarters of the cooled coconut to the yogurt, then scoop the seeds from the passion fruit over the top and lightly fold into the yogurt.

4. Layer alternate spoonfuls of strawberry and yogurt in four (1-cup) decorative jars or serving dishes, then sprinkle with the remaining coconut and the goji berries. Cover with the lid or plastic wrap and chill until ready to serve. Eat within 24 hours.

PER SERVING: 139 cal / 3.5g fat / 2.8g sat fat / 18.9g carbs / 14.5g sugar / 3g fiber / 10g protein / 40mg sodium

Healthy Nectars

Ruby Fruit Reviving Smoothie

Serves 1
Prep: 15 minutes
Cook: No cooking

1 ruby red grapefruit, zest and
   a little pith removed, seeded
   and coarsely chopped
¼ cucumber, coarsely chopped
1 cup hulled strawberries
small handful of crushed ice, optional

Simple to make, this scrumptious smoothie, full of vitamin C, is guaranteed to get you off to a great start in the morning.

1. Put the grapefruit and cucumber into a blender and process until smooth.

2. Add the strawberries and crushed ice, if using, and process until blended.

3. Pour the smoothie into a glass and serve immediately.

PER SERVING: *162 cal / 0.8g fat / 0g sat fat / 40.4g carbs / 25.5g sugar / 7.3g fiber / 3.4g protein / trace sodium*

Melon & Coconut Mock Mojito

Promote your general health and well-being with this vivid green mock mojito. It's loaded with nourishing nutrients and can be processed in minutes, providing the essential energy boost needed after a workout.

Serves 1
Prep: 15–20 minutes
Cook: No cooking

¾ cup spinach
⅔ cup coconut flesh
1 cup chilled water
⅔ cup peeled, seeded, and chopped cantaloupe
1 tablespoon chopped fresh mint
juice of ½ lime
⅓ cup peeled, pitted, and chopped mango
    plus 1 extra slice to decorate
crushed ice, to serve, optional

1. Put the spinach, coconut, and water into a blender and process until smooth.

2. Add the melon, mint, lime juice, and mango, and blend until smooth and creamy.

3. Pour the drink over crushed ice, if using, and serve immediately, decorated with a mango slice.

PER SERVING: 262 cal / 17.2g fat / 14.9g sat fat / 28g carbs / 20.3g sugar / 7.3g fiber / 3.9g protein / trace sodium

Kale, Lettuce & Avocado Juice

Serves 1
Prep: 20 minutes
Cook: No cooking

¾ cup kale
½ cup fresh flat-leaf parsley
½ romaine lettuce
3 celery stalks, halved
1 apple, halved
½ lemon
⅓ cup slivered almonds
½ avocado, peeled and pitted
small handful of crushed ice, optional

Get a good helping of fruit and vegetables in a glass with this fabulous fresh juice that is ideal for anyone needing a boost. The slivered almonds add a beneficial bonus of heart-healthy monounsaturated fat, plus vitamin E.

1. Feed the kale through a juicer, followed by the parsley and lettuce. Finally, feed two of the celery stalks and the apple and lemon through the juicer.

2. Put the slivered almonds into a blender or food processor and process until finely ground.

3. Add the juice and avocado flesh to the almonds, and process until smooth. Add the crushed ice, if using, and blend again.

4. Pour the juice into a glass. Decorate with the remaining celery stalk and serve immediately.

PER SERVING: *441 cal / 31.6g fat / 3.3g sat fat / 35.3g carbs / 14.2g sugar / 9.8g fiber / 13.9g protein / 120mg sodium*

Spinach & Melon Cooler

Antioxidant-rich spinach and vitamin-packed melon create this cleansing cooler, enhanced with the addition of fresh herbs. It's great as a refreshing fat-free beverage when your body needs reinvigorating.

Serves 1
Prep: 15 minutes
Cook: No cooking

½ Galia or honeydew melon,
    peeled, seeded, and thickly sliced
3 cups baby spinach
2 large stems of fresh
    flat-leaf parsley
3 large stems of fresh mint
small handful of ice, optional

1. Feed the melon through a juicer, followed by the spinach, parsley, and two stems of the mint.

2. Fill a glass halfway with ice, if using, then pour in the juice.

3. Decorate with the remaining stem of mint and serve immediately.

PER SERVING: 71 cal / 0.5g fat / 0g sat fat / 14.3g carbs / 11.5g sugar / 0.6g fiber / 2.2g protein / 80mg sodium

Vegetable Stomach Soothing Juice

To keep your stomach in the best of health, choose this appealing vegetable stomach soother, which is enriched with a little hemp seed oil to add an important boost of polyunsaturated fat and vitamin E.

Serves 1

Prep: 20 minutes
Cook: No cooking

3 oranges, zest and a little pith removed
1 carrot, halved
2 tomatoes, coarsely chopped
½ cup chilled water
1 small green chile, halved
2 celery stalks, thickly sliced
2 teaspoons hemp seed oil

1. Cut two oranges in half and feed them and the carrot through a juicer. Pour the juice into a blender.

2. Coarsely chop and seed the remaining orange, then put it, the tomatoes, and water into the blender and process until smooth.

3. Add the chile and celery and process again until blended. Pour the juice into a glass, stir in the hemp seed oil, and serve immediately.

Broccoli & Parsley Revitalizing Juice

Serves 1
Prep: 15 minutes
Cook: No cooking

1½ cups broccoli florets
½ cup fresh flat-leaf parsley
½ fennel bulb
2 apples, halved
chilled water, to taste, optional
small handful of ice, optional

After a weekday workout or some strenuous exercise, this vitamin- and mineral-loaded juice is guaranteed to revitalize your body quickly. It's also fat-free and free of processed sugars, making it a great alternative to carbonated energy beverages.

1. Feed the broccoli and parsley through the juicer, followed by the fennel and apples.

2. Top up the juice with chilled water to taste, if desired.

3. Fill a glass halfway with ice, if using, then pour in the juice. Serve the juice immediately.

PER SERVING: *119 cal / 0.6g fat / 0g sat fat / 27g carbs / 15.1g sugar / 0.2g fiber / 3.2g protein / 80mg sodium*

Sprout Tonic

Serves 1
Prep: 10 minutes
Cook: No cooking

4 Brussels sprouts
⅔ cup beet greens
½ cup chopped Swiss chard
1 cup unsweetened rice milk

Brussels sprouts boast vitamins, minerals, fiber, and protein in this intense, health-giving tonic that is appetizing and satisfying.

1. Put the Brussels sprouts, beet greens, and Swiss chard into a blender or food processor.

2. Pour the rice milk into the blender or food processor and blend until smooth and creamy.

3. Pour the tonic into a glass and serve immediately.

PER SERVING: *162 cal / 2.7g fat / 0g sat fat / 31.8g carbs / 15.2g sugar / 5g fiber / 4.2g protein / 200mg sodium*

Warm Arugula, Apple & Ginseng Juice

Serves 1

Prep: 10 minutes, plus infusing

Cook: No cooking

1 ginseng tea bag or 1 teaspoon ginseng loose tea

⅔ cup boiling water

1 apple, halved

1½ cups arugula

1. Put the tea into a teacup. Pour the boiling water over the top and let the mixture steep for about 4 minutes. Strain the tea into a heatproof glass or mug.

2. Feed the apple through a juicer, followed by the arugula.

3. Stir the juice into the tea in the glass and serve while it is still warm.

This revitalizing drink can also be enjoyed cold. Simply let cool, then drop in some ice cubes and stir well before serving.

PER SERVING: *48 cal / 0.3g fat / 0g sat fat / 10.4g carbs / 7.6g sugar / 0.1g fiber / 1.1g protein / trace sodium*

Protein Berry Whip

Serves 4
Prep: 10–15 minutes
Cook: No cooking

1⅓ cups frozen sliced strawberries
⅓ cup frozen blueberries
12 Brazil nuts
⅓ cup chopped cashew nuts
¼ cup rolled oats
2 cups almond milk
2 tablespoons maple syrup

1. Put the strawberries, blueberries, Brazil nuts, and cashew nuts into a blender. Sprinkle with the oats, then pour in half of the almond milk. Blend until smooth.

2. Add the remaining milk and maple syrup, and blend again until smooth.

3. Pour the berry whip into four glasses and serve immediately with spoons. As the drink stands, the blueberries will almost set the liquid, but as soon as you stir it, it will turn to liquid again.

These whips contain good amounts of protein, which is essential for the growth and repair of muscles and helps to fight infection.

PER SERVING: *209 cal / 12.8g fat / 2.4g sat fat / 21.5g carbs / 10.4g sugar / 3.6g fiber / 5g protein / 40mg sodium*

Bee Pollen & Nectarine Milk Shake

Nutritious bee pollen adds an intriguing touch to this delicious and nourishing nectarine milk shake. Milk and plain yogurt make the perfect team for creating a calcium-rich base, and the honey adds natural sweetness, too.

Serves 2

Prep: 15 minutes
Cook: No cooking

2 ripe nectarines, quartered
1 cup low-fat milk
2 tablespoons Greek-style plain yogurt
1 tablespoon bee pollen
1 teaspoon honey
handful of ice cubes
1 teaspoon bee pollen, to decorate
2 slices nectarine, to decorate

1. Put the the nectarines, milk, yogurt, bee pollen, and honey into a blender and process until smooth. Add the ice cubes and process again until completely blended.

2. Pour the milk shake into chilled glasses and decorate with the bee pollen and a fresh slice of nectarine. Serve immediately.

PER SERVING: *163 cal* / *3.2g fat* / *1.8g sat fat* / *28.7g carbs* / *22.8g sugar* / *2.6g fiber* / *7.3g protein* / *40mg sodium*

Raw Cocoa Milk Shake

Great for waking up your taste buds first thing, or for a nutritious chocolate hit any time, this delicious dairy-free and gluten-free milk shake provides the perfect pick-me-up, and it is suitable for vegetarians and vegans, too.

Serves 4
Prep: 10 minutes
Cook: No cooking

1¾ cups almond milk
3 dried pitted dates
¾ cup cashew nuts
2 tablespoons raw cocoa powder
1 teaspoon ground cinnamon
handful of ice cubes
1 tablespoon orange zest, to decorate

1. Put the almond milk, dates, cashew nuts, cocoa powder, cinnamon, and ice into a blender.

2. Blend thoroughly until the milk shake is a thick pouring consistency.

3. Pour into chilled glasses, decorate with the orange zest, and serve immediately.

PER SERVING: 198 cal / 10.8g fat / 2g sat fat / 24.9g carbs / 15.5g sugar / 3.9g fiber / 5.2g protein / 40mg sodium

Pineapple & Mint Iced Tea

This refreshing iced tea is steeped with soothing ginger and fresh mint and delivers a bounty of vitamins and minerals, making a fresh, rejuvenating beverage that is quenching at any time of the day.

Makes 2 cups

Prep: 20–25 minutes, plus steeping
Cook: 45 minutes

1 pineapple
4 cups water
⅓ bunch of fresh mint
2-inch piece of fresh ginger, finely sliced
½ cup agave syrup
crushed ice
2 tablespoons mint leaves, to decorate

1. Prepare the pineapple by slicing off the bottom and top with a sharp knife. Rest the pineapple on its bottom and slice off the peel until you reveal the flesh. Slice the fruit in half and remove the woody core that runs down the center. Cut the remaining flesh into ¾-inch cubes.

2. Pour the water into a large saucepan and add the pineapple, mint sprigs, and ginger. Stir in the agave syrup and put the saucepan over medium–high heat. Simmer for 45 minutes, or until the liquid has reduced by half.

3. Remove from the heat and let the nectar cool completely and steep. This will take 4–5 hours. Using a slotted spoon, remove the mint sprigs and ginger.

4. Put some crushed ice into the bottom of pitcher and add the fresh mint leaves on top. Pour the cooled nectar over the ice and mint and stir to mix. Serve immediately.

PER 2 CUPS: 810 cal / 1.2g fat / 0.1g sat fat / 206.8g carbs / 177.1g sugar / 13.5g fiber / 5.3g protein / trace sodium

Kiwi & Cucumber Infused Water

Makes about 6⅓ cups

Prep: 20 minutes, plus freezing
Cook: No cooking

½ cucumber
2 kiwis, peeled and thickly sliced
4 cups chilled water

Lemon ice cubes

zest of 1 lemon
water to fill an ice cube tray

Chilled water is infused with kiwi and cucumber to make this cleansing and refreshing drink. Served with zesty lemon ice cubes, it is a great thirst quencher, especially when you're feeling hot and tired.

1. Make your lemon ice cubes at least 4 hours before they are needed. Cut the lemon zest into pieces that will sit neatly in the sections of an ice cube tray. Place the zest pieces in the sections in the tray and fill the sections with water. Freeze for at least 4–6 hours, or until needed.

2. When ready to serve, peel ribbons from a cucumber, using a vegetable peeler. Place the ribbons in the bottom of a pitcher, along with the fresh kiwi slices.

3. Add the lemon zest ice cubes to the pitcher and top up with the chilled water. Serve immediately.

PER 6⅓ CUPS: *110 cal / 0.9g fat / 0.1g sat fat / 26.7g carbs / 15.1g sugar / 5.5g fiber / 2.7g protein / trace sodium*

Cardamom, Fennel & Ginger Tea

Get your day off to a great start with this fragrant and soothing low-sugar tea, steeped with spices. Ginger is a helpful digestive aid and has important anti-inflammatory properties, adding to this beneficial hot tea.

Makes 4 cups
Prep: 10–15 minutes, plus infusing
Cook: No cooking

10 green cardamom pods
1 teaspoon fennel seeds
3¼-inch piece of fresh ginger, sliced
4 cups boiling water

1. Put the cardamom pods onto a heavy cutting board and gently bruise each pod with a rolling pin.

2. Place the crushed pods into a teapot. Add the fennel seeds and fresh ginger. Pour the boiling water over the top and let steep for 5–6 minutes, or to your taste.

3. Pour the tea into mugs through a tea strainer and serve immediately.

PER 4 CUPS: 2 cal / 0g fat / 0g sat fat / 0.5g carbs / 0g sugar / 0.1g fiber / 0.1g protein / trace sodium

Homemade Masala Chai Tea

Makes 2½ cups
Prep: 15 minutes
Cook: 30–35 minutes

1 tablespoon loose Assam tea
2-inch piece of fresh ginger, grated
2 cinnamon sticks
5 black peppercorns
6 cloves
5 green cardamom pods, bashed
2 star anise
1¼ cups low-fat milk
1 tablespoon honey

Aromatic mixed spices, including ginger, cinnamon, and cloves, add a wonderful warming flavor to this restorative hot milky tea. It is naturally sweetened with honey, keeping it free from refined and processed sugar.

1. Put 1¼ cups of water into a saucepan and bring to a boil over medium heat. Stir in the Assam tea and continue to gently boil for 3–4 minutes.

2. Add the ginger, cinnamon sticks, peppercorns, cloves, cardamom, and star anise and gently simmer for 12–15 minutes. Add the milk and simmer for an additional 10 minutes.

3. Sweeten with the honey. Strain the tea and serve immediately in mugs or tall heatproof glasses.

PER 2½ CUPS: *217 cal / 5.9g fat / 3.8g sat fat / 32.5g carbs / 32.4g sugar / 0.2g fiber / 10g protein / 160mg sodium*

INDEX

almond milk 11
  Avocado Chocolate Mousse 252
  Barley Porridge with Carmelized Fruits 14
  Protein Berry Whip 301
  Raw Cocoa Milk Shake 305
almonds
  Butternut Squash & Lentil Stew 165
  Eggplants Stuffed with Bulgur Wheat 162
  Gluten & Dairy-Free Orange & Almond Cake 269
  Kale, Lettuce & Avocado Juice 291
  Mocha Soufflés with Mascarpone 262
  Roasted Kale Chips 100
  Skinny Banana Split Sundaes 255
  Spicy Rice with Chicken & Pomegranate 80
apples
  Breakfast Carrot Cake Cookies 27
  Broccoli & Parsley Revitalizing Juice 297
  Cranberry & Red Cabbage Slaw 112
  Healthy Apple Crisp 243
  Kale, Lettuce & Avocado Juice 291
  Raw Shoot & Seed-Packed Salad 159
  Roasted Pork with Gingered Apples 203
  Seed-Packed Granola 21
  Spiced Apple Whole-Wheat Cupcakes 265
  Warm Arugula, Apple & Ginseng Juice 300
apricots
  Breakfast Carrot Cake Cookies 27
  Raw Shoot & Seed-Packed Salad 159
arugula
  Lean Beef Stir-Fry 220
  Sea Bass & Trout Ceviche 66
  Tagliatelle with Roasted Pumpkin 174
  Warm Arugula, Apple & Ginseng Juice 300
  Warm Crab, Lentil & Herb Salad 228
asparagus
  Asparagus with Hot-Smoked Salmon & Poached Egg 75
  Brown Rice Risotto Primavera 173
  Miso & Tofu Salad 186
  Rainbow Nori Rolls 77
avocados
  Avocado & Cashew Nut Pasta Sauce 143
  Avocado, Bacon & Chile Frittata 93
  Avocado Chocolate Mousse 252
  Avocado, Lemon & Paprika Dressing 134
  Good-for-You Cobb Salad 88
  Guacamole Dip 146
  Jerk Chicken with Papaya & Avocado Salsa 217
  Kale & Lima Bean Casserole 178
  Kale, Lettuce & Avocado Juice 291
  Mashed Avocado & Quinoa Wrap 52
  Protein Rice Bowl 69
  Super Green Salad 55
  Turkey Wraps with Avocado Salsa 78

Baba Ghanoush 148
bacon
  Avocado, Bacon & Chile Frittata 93
  Clams in a Bacon & Leek Broth 71
  Good-for-You Cobb Salad 88

bananas
  Banana, Goji & Hazelnut Bread 46
  Barley Porridge with Carmelized Fruits 14
  Chia Seed & Banana Ice Pops 256
  Healthy French Toast with Bananas & Toasted Pecans 19
  Skinny Banana Split Sundaes 255
beans 9
  Country-Style Ham & Pinto Beans 236
  Spanish Vegetable Stew 191
  Three Bean & Chia Salad 65
  Tuna with Bok Choy & Soba Noodles 204
  Winter Squash, Feta & Adzuki Bean Packages 185
  see also black beans; fava beans; lima beans; edamame (soybeans)
bean sprouts
  Fresh Pho with Beef 60
  Miso & Tofu Salad 186
Bee Pollen & Nectarine Milk Shake 302
beef
  Fresh Pho with Beef 60
  Lean Beef Stir-fry 220
  Seared Beef Salad 84
  Slow-Cooked Beef with Mashed Lima Beans 215
  Spicy Steak with Roasted Squash 198
  Stuffed Red Bell Peppers 188
beets 11
  Beet & Cucumber Tzatziki on Salad Greens 145
  Beet & Hazelnut Pesto 144
  Beet Burgers in Buns 181
  Celebration Chocolate & Beet Cake 281
  Chicken & Giant Couscous Salad 201
  Chicken with Pomegranate & Beet Tabbouleh 231
  Rainbow Nori Rolls 77
  Red Beet Hash 39
  Roasted Beet & Squash Salad 192
  Sprout Tonic 299
bell peppers
  Black Bean & Quinoa Burritos 161
  Country-Style Ham & Pinto Beans 236
  Lean Beef Stir-Fry 220
  Rainbow Nori Rolls 77
  Spanish Vegetable Stew 191
  Spiced Turkey Stew with Couscous 208
  Stuffed Red Bell Peppers 188
black beans
  Black Bean & Date Brownies 249
  Black Bean & Quinoa Burritos 161
blackberries: Cardamom Waffles with Blackberries & Figs 34
blueberries
  Buckwheat Blinis with Pears & Blueberries 43
  Coconut & Mango Quinoa Puddings 261
  Frozen Yogurt Berries 102
  Mixed Berry Yellow Cakes 272
  Protein Berry Whip 301
  Seed-Packed Granola 21
bok choy: Tuna with Bok Choy & Soba Noodles 204

bread
  Banana, Goji & Hazelnut Bread 46
  Healthy French Toast with Bananas & Toasted Pecans 19
  Mushrooms on Rye Toast 40
  Poached Eggs & Kale with Whole-Wheat Sourdough 45
  Walnut & Seed Bread 49
broccoli
  Baby Broccoli with Pine Nuts 119
  Broccoli & Parsley Revitalizing Juice 297
  Gingered Salmon with Stir-fried Kale 210
  Super Green Salad 55
  Warm Crab, Lentil & Herb Salad 228
Brussels sprouts: Sprout Tonic 299
buckwheat 11
  Buckwheat Blinis with Pears & Blueberries 43
  Mushrooms & Squash on Buckwheat 155
bulgur wheat
  Eggplants Stuffed with Bulgur Wheat 162
  Multigrain & Seed Sprout Salad 167
butternut squash see squash

cabbage
  Pork-Stuffed Cabbage Leaves 213
  Steamed Greens with Lemon & Cilantro 125
  see also red cabbage
Caesar Dressing, Healthy 141
Caper & Oregano Vinaigrette 138
Cardamom, Fennel & Ginger Tea 313
carrots
  Breakfast Carrot Cake Cookies 27
  Brown Rice Risotto Primavera 173
  Red Cabbage, Turkey & Quinoa Pilaf 239
  Spiced Mashed Carrot 109
  Tuna & Wasabi Burgers 233
  Vegetable Stomach Soothing Juice 294
cauliflower
  Basil & Lemon Cauliflower Rice 114
  Cranberry & Red Cabbage Slaw 112
  Whole Baked Cauliflower 170
celery
  Basil & Lemon Cauliflower Rice 114
  Kale, Lettuce & Avocado Juice 291
  Vegetable Stomach Soothing Juice 294
Chai Tea Cookies 259
cheese
  Black Bean & Quinoa Burritos 161
  Shrimp-Filled Baked Sweet Potatoes 87
  Squash, Chorizo & Goat Cheese Quiche 82
  see also cream cheese; feta cheese; Parmesan cheese; ricotta cheese
chia seeds 11
  Chia Seed & Banana Ice Pops 256
  Chocolate & Chia Puddings 279
  Cranberry & Red Cabbage Slaw 112
  Fig & Oat Bites 96
  Greek-Style Yogurt with Orange Zest & Toasted Seeds 17
  Jerk Chicken with Papaya & Avocado Salsa 217
  Three Bean & Chia Salad 65

chicken
    Chicken & Giant Couscous Salad 201
    Chicken with Pomegranate & Beet
       Tabbouleh 231
    Jerk Chicken with Papaya & Avocado Salsa
       217
    Spicy Rice with Chicken & Pomegranate
       80
chickpeas
    Basil & Raw Garlic Hummus 149
    Cashew & Chickpea Curry 169
    Smoky Paprika Roasted Chickpeas 103
    Stuffed Red Bell Peppers 188
    Sweet Potato Falafels 110
chocolate
    Avocado Chocolate Mousse 252
    Black Bean & Date Brownies 249
    Celebration Chocolate & Beet Cake 281
    Chocolate & Chia Puddings 279
    Coconut, Cacao & Hazelnut Truffles 277
    Date Power Balls 105
    Homemade Cacao & Hazelnut Butter 33
    Mocha Soufflés with Mascarpone 262
    Raw Cocoa Milk Shake 305
    Skinny Banana Split Sundaes 255
Clams in a Bacon & Leek Broth 71
coconut
    Breakfast Carrot Cake Cookies 27
    Cashew & Chickpea Curry 169
    Chocolate & Chia Puddings 279
    Coconut & Mango Quinoa Puddings 261
    Coconut, Cacao & Hazelnut Truffles 277
    Coconut Milk, Strawberry & Honey Ice
       Cream 247
    Date Power Balls 105
    Melon & Coconut Mock Mojito 288
    Passion Fruit & Strawberry Yogurts 282
coconut oil 11
    Black Bean & Date Brownies 249
    Breakfast Carrot Cake Cookies 27
    Fig & Oat Bites 96
    Healthy Apple Crisp 243
coconut water 11
corn
    Shrimp-Filled Baked Sweet Potatoes 87
    Three Bean & Chia Salad 65
couscous
    Chicken & Giant Couscous Salad 201
    Spiced Turkey Stew with Couscous 208
crabmeat: Warm Crab, Lentil & Herb
    Salad 228
cranberries
    Cranberry & Red Cabbage Slaw 112
    Red Cabbage, Turkey & Quinoa Pilaf 239
    Seed-Packed Granola 21
cream cheese
    Mocha Soufflés with Mascarpone 262
    Tofu Lemon Cheesecake 251
cucumber
    Beet & Cucumber Tzatziki on Salad
       Leaves 145
    Kiwi & Cucumber Infused Water 311
    Ruby Fruit Reviving Smoothie 287
    Tuna & Wasabi Burgers 233

date syrup
    Cinnamon Crepes with Tropical Fruit
       Salad 24
    Smoky Paprika Roasted Chickpeas 103
dates
    Raw Cocoa Milk Shake 305
    Tofu Lemon Cheesecake 251
    see also Medjool dates

edamame (soybeans)
    Three Bean & Chia Salad 65
    Vietnamese Tofu & Noodle Salad 91
eggplants
    Baba Ghanoush 148
    Eggplants Stuffed with Bulgur Wheat
       162
    Spanish Vegetable Stew 191
eggs
    Asparagus with Hot-Smoked Salmon &
       Poached Egg 75
    Avocado, Bacon & Chile Frittata 93
    Cardamom Waffles with Blackberries &
       Figs 34
    Good-for-You Cobb Salad 88
    Healthy French Toast with Bananas &
       Toasted Pecans 19
    High-Fiber Green Lentil & Egg Salad 177
    Poached Eggs & Kale with Whole-Wheat
       Sourdough 45
    Protein Rice Bowl 69
    Red Beet Hash 39
    Spinach & Nutmeg Baked Eggs 23
    Squash, Chorizo & Goat Cheese Quiche 82
    Three Herb & Ricotta Omelet 30
    Whole-Wheat Spinach, Pea & Feta Tart 57

farro
    Mushroom Farro Risotto 194
    Roasted Beet & Squash Salad 192
fava beans
    Chilled Fava Bean Soup 63
    Fava Bean & Mint Hummus with
       Vegetable Sticks 151
feta cheese
    Eggplants Stuffed with Bulgur Wheat
       162
    Winter Squash, Feta & Adzuki Bean
       Packages 185
    Whole-Wheat Spinach, Pea & Feta Tart 57
    Zucchini Spaghetti 157
figs
    Cardamom Waffles with Blackberries &
       Figs 34
    Coconut, Cacao & Hazelnut Truffles 277
    Fig & Oat Bites 96
    Gluten & Dairy-Free Orange & Almond
       Cake 269
fish and seafood
    Clams in a Bacon & Leek Broth 71
    Monkfish in Pesto & Prosciutto with
       Ricotta Spinach 223
    Scallops with Pea Puree 219
    Sea Bass & Trout Ceviche 66
    Shrimp-Filled Baked Sweet Potatoes 87
    Squid with Saffron Mayonnaise 207

Warm Crab, Lentil & Herb Salad 228
    see also salmon; tuna
flaxseed 11
    Breakfast Carrot Cake Cookies 27
    Date Power Balls 105

Garlic & Jalapeño Dipping Oil 135
Ginger, Garlic & Soy Dressing 128
Gluten- & Dairy-Free Orange & Almond
    Cake 269
goji berries 11
    Banana, Goji & Hazelnut Bread 46
    Date Power Balls 105
    Passion Fruit & Strawberry
       Yogurts 282
    Seared Beef Salad 84
grapefruit
    Cinnamon Crepes with Tropical Fruit
       Salad 24
    Ruby Fruit Reviving Smoothie 287
    Sea Bass & Trout Ceviche 66
green beans
    Roasted Pork with Gingered Apples 203
    Three Bean & Chia Salad 65
Green Tea Fruit Salad 244
Guacamole Dip 146

ham
    Country-Style Ham & Pinto Beans 236
    Monkfish in Pesto & Prosciutoo with
       Ricotta Spinach 223
hazelnuts
    Banana, Goji & Hazelnut Bread 46
    Basil & Lemon Cauliflower Rice 114
    Beet & Hazelnut Pesto 144
    Buckwheat Blinis with Pears &
       Blueberries 43
    Coconut, Cacao & Hazelnut Truffles 277
    Coconut Milk, Strawberry & Honey Ice
       Cream 247
    Homemade Cacao & Hazelnut Butter 33

Jerusalem artichokes: Red Beet Hash 39

kale 11
    Gingered Salmon with Stir-Fried Kale 210
    Kale & Lima Bean Casserole 178
    Kale, Lettuce & Avocado Juice 291
    Poached Eggs & Kale with Whole-Wheat
       Sourdough 45
    Pork Medallions with Pomegranate 234
    Rainbow Nori Rolls 77
    Roasted Kale Chips 100
    Seared Beef Salad 84
    Super Green Salad 55
kiwi
    Green Tea Fruit Salad 244
    Kiwi & Cucumber Infused Water 311

Lamb & Spinach Meatballs 225
leeks
    Brown Rice Risotto Primavera 173
    Clams in a Bacon & Leek Broth 71
    Gingered Salmon with Stir-Fried Kale 210
    High-Fiber Green Lentil & Egg Salad 177

lentils
Butternut Squash & Lentil Stew 165
High-Fiber Green Lentil & Egg Salad 177
Stuffed Red Bell Peppers 188
Warm Crab, Lentil & Herb Salad 228
lima beans
Kale & Lima Bean Casserole 178
Slow-Cooked Beef with Mashed Lima
Beans 215
Whole Baked Cauliflower 170

mangoes
Cinnamon Crepes with Tropical Fruit
Salad 24
Coconut & Mango Quinoa Puddings 261
Fruity Ice Pops 270
Green Tea Fruit Salad 244
Melon & Coconut Mock Mojito 288
Shrimp-Filled Baked Sweet Potatoes 87
Medjool dates 11
Black Bean & Date Brownies 249
Date Power Balls 105
melon
Melon & Coconut Mock Mojito 288
Spinach & Melon Cooler 293
see also watermelon
millet: Beet Burgers in Buns 181
miso
Lime & Miso Dressing 136
Miso & Tofu Salad 186
Mocha Soufflés with Mascarpone 262
Monkfish in Pesto & Prosciutto with
Ricotta Spinach 223
mushrooms
Lean Beef Stir-Fry 220
Mushroom Farro Risotto 194
Mushrooms & Squash on Buckwheat 155
Mushrooms on Rye Toast 40
Spicy Steak with Roasted Squash
198

nectarines: Bee Pollen & Nectarine Milk Shake
302
noodles
Fresh Pho with Beef 60
Tuna with Bok Choy & Soba Noodles 204
Vietnamese Tofu & Noodle Salad 91
nuts 8
Avocado & Cashew Nut Pasta Sauce 143
Breakfast Carrot Cake Cookies 27
Brown Rice with Pistachio Nuts, Parsley &
Dried Cherries 123
Cashew & Chickpea Curry 169
Cinnamon Crepes with Tropical Fruit
Salad 24
Date Power Balls 105
Green Tea Fruit Salad 244
Healthy Apple Crisp 243
Healthy French Toast with Bananas &
Toasted Pecans 19
Honey & Spice Snacking Nuts 99
Protein Berry Whip 301
Protein Rice Bowl 69
Raw Cocoa Milk Shake 305
Red Cabbage, Turkey & Quinoa Pilaf 239

Tofu Lemon Cheesecake 251
see also almonds; hazelnuts; walnuts

oats
Barley Porridge with Carmelized Fruits 14
Breakfast Carrot Cake Cookies 27
Fig & Oat Bites 96
Healthy Apple Crisp 243
Protein Berry Whip 301
Seed-Packed Granola 21
Orzo with Mint & Fresh Tomatoes 117

papayas
Barley Porridge with Carmelized Fruits 14
Green Tea Fruit Salad 244
Jerk Chicken with Papaya & Avocado Salsa
217
Parmesan cheese
Avocado & Cashew Nut Pasta Sauce 143
Beet & Hazelnut Pesto 144
Brown Rice Risotto Primavera 173
Mushroom Farro Risotto 194
Sprouting Broccoli with Pine Nuts 119
Tagliatelle with Roasted Pumpkin 174
Passion Fruit & Strawberry Yogurts 282
pasta
Avocado & Cashew Nut Pasta Sauce 143
Orzo with Mint & Fresh Tomatoes 117
Slow-Cooked Tomato Pasta Sauce 142
Tagliatelle with Roasted Pumpkin 174
pastry
Squash, Chorizo & Goat Cheese Quiche 82
Whole-Wheat Spinach, Pea & Feta Tart 57
Winter Squash, Feta & Adzuki Bean
Packages 185
peaches: Barley Porridge with Carmelized
Fruits 14
pears
Buckwheat Blinis with Pears &
Blueberries 43
Green Tea Fruit Salad 244
peas
Scallops with Pea Puree 219
Whole-Wheat Spinach, Pea & Feta
Tart 57
see also snow pea
peppers see bell peppers
pineapple
Cinnamon Crepes with Tropical Fruit
Salad 24
Pineapple & Mint Iced Tea 308
pomegranates 11
Chicken & Giant Couscous Salad 201
Chicken with Pomegranate & Beet
Tabbouleh 231
Eggplants Stuffed with Bulgur Wheat
162
Green Tea Fruit Salad 244
Pork Medallions with Pomegranate 234
Spicy Rice with Chicken & Pomegranate
80
pork
Pork Medallions with Pomegranate 234
Pork-Stuffed Cabbage Leaves 213
Roasted Pork with Gingered Apples 203

potatoes
Cashew & Chickpea Curry 169
Spanish Vegetable Stew 191
pumpkin and pumpkin/pepita seeds
Butternut Wedges with Sage & Pumpkin
Seeds 108
Squash & Pepita Muffins 37
Tagliatelle with Roasted Pumpkin 174
see also squash

quinoa 11
Black Bean & Quinoa Burritos 161
Coconut & Mango Quinoa Puddings 261
Mashed Avocado & Quinoa Wrap 52
Multigrain & Seed Sprout Salad 167
Red Cabbage, Turkey & Quinoa Pilaf 239

radishes
Beet & Cucumber Tzatziki on Salad
Greens 145
Seared Beef Salad 84
Tuna & Wasabi Burgers 233
raspberries
Frozen Yogurt Berries 102
Mixed Berry Yellow Cakes 272
Raspberry & Watermelon Sorbet 274
red cabbage
Cranberry & Red Cabbage Slaw 112
Mashed Avocado & Quinoa Wrap 52
Red Cabbage, Turkey & Quinoa Pilaf 239
rice
Brown Rice Risotto Primavera 173
Brown Rice with Pistachio Nuts, Parsley &
Dried Cherries 123
Cashew & Chickpea Curry 169
Country-Style Ham & Pinto Beans 236
Good-for-You Cobb Salad 88
Multigrain & Seed Sprout Salad 167
Pork-Stuffed Cabbage Leaves 213
Protein Rice Bowl 69
Rainbow Nori Rolls 77
Roasted Beet & Squash Salad 192
Spicy Rice with Chicken & Pomegranate
80
ricotta cheese
Flatbread Pizza with Zucchini Ribbons 72
Monkfish in Pesto & Proscuitto with Ricotta
Spinach 223
Three Herb & Ricotta Omelet 30

salmon
Asparagus with Hot-Smoked Salmon &
Poached Egg 75
Gingered Salmon with Stir-Fried Kale 210
Scallops with Pea Puree 219
Sea Bass & Trout Ceviche 66
seeds 8
Butternut Wedges with Sage & Pumpkin
Seeds 108
Date Power Balls 105
Greek-Style Yogurt with Orange Zest &
Toasted Seeds 17
Honey & Spice Snacking Nuts 99
Lime & Miso Dressing 136
Miso & Tofu Salad 186

Raw Shoot & Seed-Packed Salad 159
Rosemary, Sea Salt & Sesame Popcorn 107
Seed-Packed Granola 21
Squash & Pepita Muffins 37
Super Green Salad 55
Sweet Potato Falafels 110
Vietnamese Tofu & Noodle Salad 91
Walnut & Seed Bread 49
Zucchini Spaghetti 157
see also chia seeds; flaxseed; seed and
bean sprouts
seed sprouts
Miso & Tofu Salad 186
Multigrain & Seed Sprout
Salad 167
Raw Shoot & Seed-Packed Salad 159
see also bean sprouts
Shrimp-Filled Baked Sweet Potatoes 87
snow peas
Fresh Pho with Beef 60
Lean Beef Stir-fry 220
Miso & Tofu Salad 186
Vietnamese Tofu & Noodle Salad 91
see also peas
spinach
Chicken with Pomegranate & Beet
Tabbouleh 231
High-fiber Green Lentil & Egg Salad 177
Jerk Chicken with Papaya & Avocado Salsa
217
Lamb & Spinach Meatballs 225
Mashed Avocado & Quinoa Wrap 52
Melon & Coconut Mock Mojito 288
Monkfish in Pesto & Proscuitto with Ricotta
Spinach 223
Mushroom Farro Risotto 194
Orzo with Mint & Fresh Tomatoes 117
Protein Rice Bowl 69
Spinach & Melon Cooler 293
Spinach & Nutmeg Baked Eggs 23
Steamed Greens with Lemon & Cilantro
125
Super Green Salad 55
Whole-Wheat Spinach, Pea & Feta Tart 57
spirulina 11
squash
Butternut Squash & Lentil Stew 165
Butternut Wedges with Sage & Pumpkin
Seeds 108
Mushrooms & Squash on Buckwheat 155
Roasted Beet & Squash Salad 192
Spicy Steak with Roasted Squash
198
Squash & Pepita Muffins 37
Squash, Chorizo & Goat Cheese Quiche 82
Winter Squash, Feta & Adzuki Bean
Packages 185
see also pumpkin
Squid with Saffron Mayonnaise 207
strawberries
Coconut Milk, Strawberry & Honey Ice
Cream 247
Fruity Ice Pops 270
Mixed Berry Yellow Cakes 272
Passion Fruit & Strawberry Yogurts 282

Protein Berry Whip 301
Ruby Fruit Reviving Smoothie 287
superfoods 10–11
sweet potatoes
Red Beet Hash 39
Shrimp-Filled Baked Sweet Potatoes 87
Sweet Potato Falafels 110
Swiss chard
Sprout Tonic 299
Vietnamese Tofu & Noodle Salad 91

Tagliatelle with Roasted Pumpkin 174
tahini
Baba Ghanoush 148
Basil & Raw Garlic Hummus 149
Tahini & Lemon Dressing 130
tea
Cardamom, Fennel & Ginger Tea 313
Chai Tea Cookies 259
Green Tea Fruit Salad 244
Homemade Masala Chai Tea 315
Pineapple & Mint Iced Tea 308
Warm Arugula, Apple & Ginseng
Juice 300
tofu
Miso & Tofu Salad 186
Tofu Lemon Cheesecake 251
Vietnamese Tofu & Noodle Salad 91
tomatoes
Black Bean & Quinoa Burritos 161
Chicken & Giant Couscous Salad 201
Chicken with Pomegranate & Beet
Tabbouleh 231
Flatbread Pizza with Zucchini Ribbons 72
Good-for-You Cobb Salad 88
Kale & Lima Bean Casserole 178
Lamb & Spinach Meatballs 225
Orzo with Mint & Fresh Tomatoes 117
Pork-Stuffed Cabbage Leaves 213
Shrimp-Filled Baked Sweet Potatoes 87
Slow-Cooked Beef with Mashed Lima
Beans 215
Slow-Cooked Tomato Pasta Sauce 142
Spanish Vegetable Stew 191
Spiced Turkey Stew with Couscous 208
Stuffed Red Bell Peppers 188
Turkey Wraps with Avocado Salsa 78
Vegetable Stomach Soothing Juice 294
Whole Baked Cauliflower 170
Whole-Wheat Spinach, Pea & Feta
Tart 57
Zucchini Spaghetti 157
tortillas
Black Bean & Quinoa Burritos 161
Mashed Avocado & Quinoa Wrap 52
Turkey Wraps with Avocado Salsa 78
trout: Sea Bass & Trout Ceviche 66
tuna
Tuna & Wasabi Burgers 233
Tuna with Bok Choy & Soba Noodles 204
turkey
Red Cabbage, Turkey & Quinoa
Pilaf 239
Spiced Turkey Stew with Couscous 208
Turkey Wraps with Avocado Salsa 78

walnuts
Beet Burgers in Buns 181
Cranberry & Red Cabbage Slaw 112
Mushrooms & Squash on Buckwheat 155
Pork Medallions with Pomegranate 234
Raw Shoot & Seed-Packed Salad 159
Tagliatelle with Roasted Pumpkin 174
Walnut & Seed Bread 49
wasabi
Tuna & Wasabi Burgers 233
Wasabi & Soy Dressing 137
watercress
Basil & Lemon Cauliflower Rice 114
Good-for-You Cobb Salad 88
Tuna & Wasabi Burgers 233
watermelon
Green Tea Fruit Salad 244
Raspberry & Watermelon Sorbet 274
wheat berries
Chicken with Pomegranate & Beet
Tabbouleh 231
Pork Medallions with Pomegranate 234
wheatgrass 11

yogurt
Frozen Yogurt Berries 102
Fruity Ice Pops 270
Greek-Style Yogurt with Orange Zest &
Toasted Seeds 17
Passion Fruit & Strawberry Yogurts 282

zucchini
Beet Burgers in Buns 181
Brown Rice Risotto Primavera 173
Flatbread Pizza with Zucchini Ribbons 72
Miso & Tofu Salad 186
Multigrain & Seed Sprout Salad 167
Spanish Vegetable Stew 191
Zucchini Spaghetti 157